PROVENCE

John Flower

PROVENCE

Photography by Charlie Waite

SALEM HOUSE
TOPSFIELD MASSACHUSETTS

Photographer's note
Charlie Waite would like to thank his
wife Jessica for her loving understanding.

Library of Congress Cataloging-in-Publication Data
Flower. J. E. (John Ernest)
Provence.
''Photography by Charlie Waite'': p.
Includes index.
1. Provence (France)—Description and travel—
Guide-books. 2. Provence (France)—Description
and travel—Views. I. Waite, Charlie. II. Title.
DC611.P958F49 1987 914.4'904838 86-31446
ISBN 0-88162-276-1

Text © John Flower 1987
Photographs © Charlie Waite 1987

First published by George Philip,
27a Floral Street, London WC2E 9DP

First published in the USA by Salem House, 1987
462 Boston Street, Topsfield, MA 01983, USA

Printed in Italy

Half-title illustration **Provençal bonnets at Le Castellet.**

Title-page illustration **Trimmed vines and** *cabanon.*

Contents

Preface

My relationship with Provence began when I was a student at the University of Aix in the early 1960s. Ever since I have been regularly drawn back, not only to re-experience the delights of Provençal life but to discover new ones, hitherto unknown. This book attempts to impart something of my own enthusiasm and good fortune – though it does not give away every secret. In writing it I have been enormously fortunate in receiving help and advice from dozens of friends, chance acquaintances and the staff of countless syndicats d'initiatives and offices de tourisme. Some appear, in disguised form, and to them all – too numerous to name individually – my gratitude is sincere. It would none the less be remiss of me not to record my thanks in particular to: Andrew Best for his continuing encouragement; Lydia Greeves for her meticulous editorial assistance; Lorraine Dent for her word-processing skills; Isabel, Andrew, Christopher and Stephen for their forbearance and affectionate support; and finally, though by no means least, *tous mes amis auriolais*.

John Flower
Exeter, 1986

Spring at Malijai with the hills still brown from late frosts.

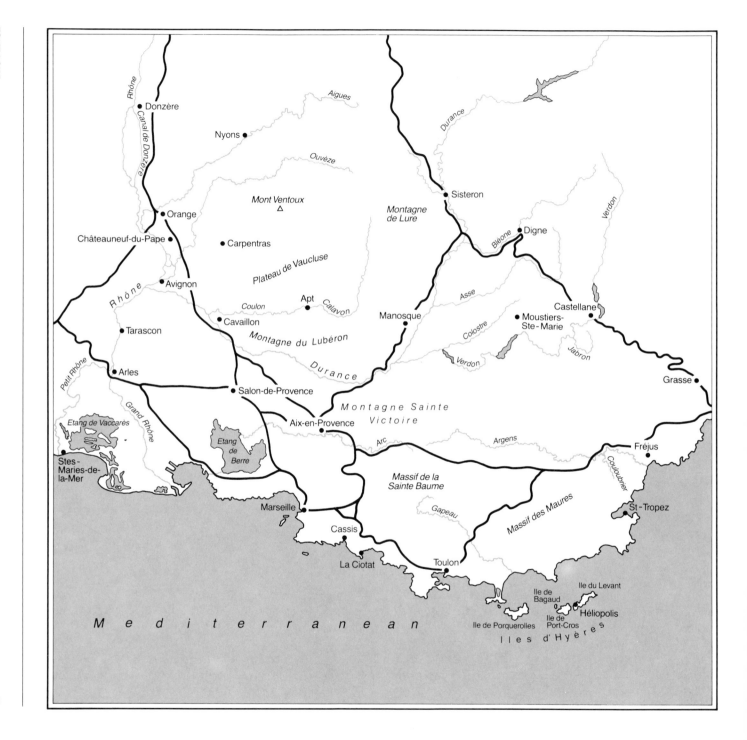

Introduction

I wander aimlessly from lane to lane,
bending a careful ear to ancient times:
the same cicadas sang in Caesar's reign,
upon the wall the same sun clings and climbs.

Provence, Vladimir Nabokov

For many people in the late twentieth century, Provence is a land of sea, sun and cicadas. Few would find themselves agreeing with the nineteenth-century English writer Tobias Smollett, who called it an 'asthmatic and blustering country'. Instead they view it, hopefully, as an opportunity to escape from the unreliable and often dreary summers of northern Europe. Even if Marseille is dismissed, somewhat unfairly, as sprawling, dirty and industrial, the names of Saint-Tropez or Le Lavandou instantly evoke pine-fringed beaches. Avignon has its bridge, Aix its fountains and the Camargue its horses. The lure of the holiday brochure is as powerful as that of the sun and during the summer months over three million visitors pour into Provence to fill roads, beaches, camp-sites and holiday homes. Yet such a view is inevitably limited. Provence defies facile stereotyping. In terms of climate, scenery, history and culture, it is one of the most varied and fascinating of all France's provinces.

The precise area covered by Provence is not easily defined and stirs even the Provençaux themselves to heated discussion. On its western flank the Rhône marks a natural boundary, as do the mountains of the Baronnies range to the north. But to the east there is a problem. For many, Provence blends into the Côte d'Azur, embracing Cannes and Nice and even extending as far as the Italian border. For some,

including many local people, the Var river which runs into the Mediterranean just west of Nice is the true boundary. Then again, some prefer the Route Napoléon (N85). This road more or less follows the path of Napoleon on his march to Paris in 1815 as it rises from Grasse to Sisteron by way of Castellane. But though less well-defined, the boundary assumed in this book is a natural dividing line which lies slightly west of the Route Napoléon. From the great ancient Roman port of Fréjus, it runs north through the hills to Fayence and thence to Castellane, Digne and Sisteron.

Evidence of human presence in Provence, in the form of rock carvings, remains of primitive settlements and skeletons, dates from over a quarter of a million years ago. The museum at Sault in particular has an interesting and informative collection. Until the Romans arrived in the second century BC, the area was populated by a large number of nomadic tribes, most notably the Ligurians who came from the east and the Celts from the north. Phoenicians and Greeks came across the sea to trade and in some places penetrated well inland to establish prosperous communities. In 218 BC Hannibal passed through on his way to attack Rome. The area was eventually brought under one authority and organized on a large scale by the Romans in the second century BC and they were to remain in power for six hundred years. There is abundant evidence of this Roman presence, including some magnificent monuments, and many more remains from this era are known still to lie buried. Major roads were built across the Provincia Romana as it was known. Parts of two in particular can still be seen: the Via Aurelia from Rome, which passed through Fréjus, Aix and Salon, a line followed more or less by the N7 today, and the Via Agrippa which led north from Arles to Avignon, Orange and Saint-Paul-Trois-Châteaux. The most flourishing period of this occupation was the reign of Augustus in the latter half of the first century BC, when both trade and the arts expanded considerably. From the Romans as well came the language from which Provençal is derived. Like many regional languages, it struggles to exist in the twentieth century, but learned societies and clubs manage to keep it alive and it is still spoken by elderly people in some of the more remote villages.

In the fifth century much of Roman Provence was ravaged by the marauding Visigoths; four hundred years later it was the turn of the Saracens, who were only finally defeated in 972 by the Franks. Thereafter and through the Middle Ages the country was never at peace. Communities developed in places which were easy to defend, notably on hilltops (*villages perchés*). The general atmosphere of hostility at this time is also commemorated in the word *défends*, which frequently appears in the names of forests or hills. By the thirteenth century order began to be re-established, largely as a result of careful intermarriage; in 1246 Charles of Anjou became Charles I of Provence and King of Sicily. Two hundred years later his descendant René, immortalized by his statue in Aix, was a major civilizing influence and instrumental in bringing much culture to the region.

During the medieval and early modern period Provence flourished. The general prosperity and the wealth and importance of individual families are reflected in the many châteaux, some of which are remarkably well preserved and still inhabited. Often these are little more than large substantial houses, usually rectangular with rounded towers at the corners. At the end of the sixteenth century, the Provençal parliament decided that such towers were both pretentious and aggressive and decreed that they should be cut down to the level of the main roof! The stunted results of such mutilation – known as *poivrières*, or pepper pots – are not always agreeable. The whole edifice was usually roofed with the large, traditional rounded tiles, *tuiles rondes* or *tuiles romaines*, still copied in much modern building. It is to this period as well that we owe so many of Provence's exquisite romanesque churches and also the growth of most of the popular religious stories, such as the one featuring Saintes-Maries-de-la-Mer. It was during the fourteenth century too that the popes came to Avignon.

Provence's history continued to be turbulent to the present day. The sixteenth century witnessed the brutality of the Wars of Religion between Catholics and Protestants, the latter being massacred in great numbers. One notorious figure from this period is the Baron des Adrets, whose bloody and brutal treatment of both Protestants and Catholics is legendary throughout the region, even if the stories told about him today owe something to exaggeration and added colour. In the early eighteenth century the plague struck, brought by trading ships from the east. Tens of thousands of people died, communities disappeared and strict precautions were taken – including the building of a plague wall – to keep the disease at bay. Traces of this wall can still be seen near Venasque and Murs in the Vaucluse. With the 1789 Revolution Provence's independence was lost and the first *départements* were created: Bouches-du-Rhône, Var and Basses-Alpes. The Vaucluse was added shortly afterwards when Papal interests were sold.

Throughout the nineteenth and twentieth centuries the pattern has been much the same. Industrial development and especially tourism have undoubtedly brought some prosperity. But there have also been upheavals and troubles. Local feelings have often run counter to those of central government;

Springtime in the valley of the Jabron, looking north from near Noyers.

World War I drained the region of much of its manpower with harmful effects on its economy; the Germans invaded from North Africa in 1942; in the mid 1950s tens of thousands of refugees arrived from Algeria. Some locals still complain of neglect and a lack of financial support, but in 1956 Provence (with the Côte d'Azur and Corsica) was designated as a new economic region. In some ways the attempt to bring new industries to Provence has been successful: hydro-electric schemes, atomic research stations and ship-building have all stimulated wealth and employment. But the beneficial effects have been felt only in relatively small areas, such as the Rhône valley or La Ciotat and Toulon. Provence still depends heavily on agriculture and therefore on the weather.

Again the popular image is limited and misleading. Certainly a combination of long, hot summers, mild winters and carefully controlled irrigation has produced ideal growing conditions in some places. From spring to late autumn market stalls display a bright and succulent array of fruit and vegetables – huge dark cherries, bright green apples and plums, brilliant red peppers and purple aubergines. In some places two crops a year are normal. Wine, some of it too good to export, is made enthusiastically, both by individual growers (*vignerons*) and in local co-operatives. But the weather can be treacherous. Long periods of drought, violent storms, hail and even severe frosts can cause extensive and costly damage. And the rich soil, every bit as necessary as reliable weather, is relatively scarce. Much of Provence is covered by forest (often impenetrable by car and sadly the victim of an increasing number of fires), by the *garrigue*, or by vast mountain grasslands. Of these the *garrigue* is the most inhospitable, a semi-desert of rock and coarse soil which supports little more than spiny, aromatic plants. The grasslands, however, provide testing but superb walking country, especially in the northeast. Fortunately, the walker is well provided for. Several tracks belonging to the system known as the *Grandes Randonnées* cross Provence and are supplemented by departmental and local paths. All are colour-coded, so that they are easy to follow. Fire paths too can provide access to the heart of some of the forested areas, but to stray from any of these can be dangerous. At the height of summer local decrees often forbid access altogether, so great is the fear of fire. At such times fire-patrols and helicopters keep a permanent watch and a failure to obey a decree can result in an instant fine.

Forest, *garrigue* and grasslands alike are best explored in the winter or spring when Provençal light is often at its most brilliant. To be alone in the middle of the Massif des Maures or on the uplands around Valensole at such times is to experience an atmosphere quite different from the one which prevails during the summer months. Then, in contrast to so many visitors, the Provençaux flee the sun and stay indoors, especially from midday to late afternoon. Shutters remain closed and the shade provided so effectively by tall buildings and narrow streets in the villages is quickly appreciated. And no visitor to Provence will remain unaware of the mistral for long. This wind, whose name derives from *mestre*, the Provençal for master, is sucked down the Rhône valley whenever a depression develops over the Mediterranean. Many Provençaux will tell you that any wind which suddenly develops is the mistral, irrespective of its direction, but the real thing is unmistakable. It is violent, cold, disagreeable and can blow for days.

Villages provide protection against it just as they do against the sun, but isolated buildings such as the *mas* and *bastides* scattered across the countryside are less fortunate. The *mas*, often farmsteads of substantial size and importance, are low buildings with shallow roofs, usually facing south or southeast to benefit from the maximum amount of sun in winter and to offer resistance to the mistral. *Bastides* are somewhat grander. Many were built in the seventeenth and eighteenth centuries as country retreats for the wealthy upper classes of Marseille and Aix. They are usually rectangular in shape and of three storeys. The

The roads north from Saint-Vincent lead into the distant hills and disappear.

Digine.

walls are thick (often more than a metre) and rendered with plaster, which was once traditionally brushed on with thyme branches (*enduit à la férigoulo*). Many *bastides* are still privately owned, some serving as farmhouses or as wine châteaux, but not a few are abandoned and falling into ruins.

Although grants are available, the restoration and upkeep of such buildings is an expensive business, and many country dwellers have moved into towns or large villages. Here controls on the renovation of old houses are now quite strict, but many new developments, especially along the popular coastal strip, have been allowed to go forward with inadequate thought or planning. A token attempt is often made to create an authentic style with beams, rough plaster finish and *tuiles romaines*. But all too frequently the results are not happy. Colours can be garish and beams can be made of plastic, while the traditional delicate edge to a roof formed from several layers of overlapping tiles protruding beyond the walls (known as *génoise*) may be crudely reproduced in

14

concrete. Too often trees have been destroyed and houses packed together on crowded sites by developers in search of a quick profit. Carnoux, populated almost entirely by people who have returned from North Africa, is a good example. In contrast, many who have come to Provence from abroad or elsewhere in France in search of a second home, a *résidence secondaire*, are careful in the work they do. It may take a long time for them to be accepted by local people, but without their efforts many villages would be far less well restored than they actually are.

If climate and landscape are all too readily stereotyped, so too are the Provençaux themselves. The popularised view of them created through Fernandel's film interpretations of Marcel Pagnol's characters is misleading. The local people will willingly grant a superficial friendship to anyone who is prepared to make the effort and accept them on their terms. But it is difficult for outsiders to gain real acceptance. The Provençaux are private, shy, and often suspicious of newcomers. Once you are accepted, however, the warmth and hospitality of their welcome is genuine. Although often frugal themselves, they will, when the occasion demands, produce some of the dishes for which Provence is renowned. Rich vegetable soups, dark stews tasting of herbs and wine, delicately roasted lamb or pheasants and fresh chickens stuffed with thyme and rosemary. Fish is plentiful and popular. *Bouillabaisse* is the most famous fish-based dish which, in its *true* form, contains the local so-called rock fish (*poissons des roches*) in quantity, cooked with onions, garlic and tomatoes. It should be eaten with oven-dried bread. *Bourride* is more common. Ideally this should contain bass, bream or grey mullet and is cooked and served with *aïoli*, the rich sauce made from eggs, garlic and olive oil. And no meal will be complete without sampling some of the many cheeses produced in Provence, especially those made from goat's milk (though genuine, pure ones are not easy to find), and the local wine, which often has an astonishing strength and depth of flavour. But it is not so much the number of individual local dishes which makes Provençal cooking so tasty and attractive. Rather it is the judicious use of herbs, olives, garlic and oil which can turn even the most ordinary of meals into something quite distinctive. Nor should *pastis* be forgotten. Few drinks are better suited to a hot climate than this aniseed-based liqueur diluted with water. But few are more treacherously powerful.

In many ways an ideal way to savour the atmosphere of Provence is simply to sit at a table on the terrace of a village café shaded by plane trees on a warm early summer's day. Life appears leisurely. *Pétanque*, the French version of bowls and a game of considerable skill, is a constant pastime. Competitions (*concours de boules*) are numerous and are accompanied by illegal betting, often involving large sums. And yet while such a cameo of village life is certainly more authentic than much that is put on to catch the tourist, it is only a glimpse of one aspect of Provence, as are the fish market at Marseille, the eerie ruins of Les Baux or a chance meeting with a shepherd on a remote northern pasture. The novelist Jean Giono, who spent his entire life in and around Manosque, once remarked that even after sixty years his own region still held mysteries for him.

When Vincent Van Gogh came to Provence in the late nineteenth century he did so for the light. Other painters have done likewise, including Picasso and Chagall. Writers too have come, some to stay, attracted by the climate or by the atmosphere of an area rich in legend: Stendhal, Kipling, Katherine Mansfield, Camus, Lawrence Durrell. . . . Nor is Provence without its own creative artists. These include Cézanne and Frédéric Mistral, a genuine Provençal writer who was awarded the Nobel Prize for Literature in 1904 or, more recently, Marcel Pagnol and Giono. For them and others the attractions of Provence are endless. They will prove to be so too for anyone with the patience to listen and observe.

* * *

Although more detailed maps exist, especially for experienced walkers, those of the series *Carte Topographique* published by the Institut national géographique are recommended. The numbers of those covering Provence are 60, 61, 66, 67 and 68.

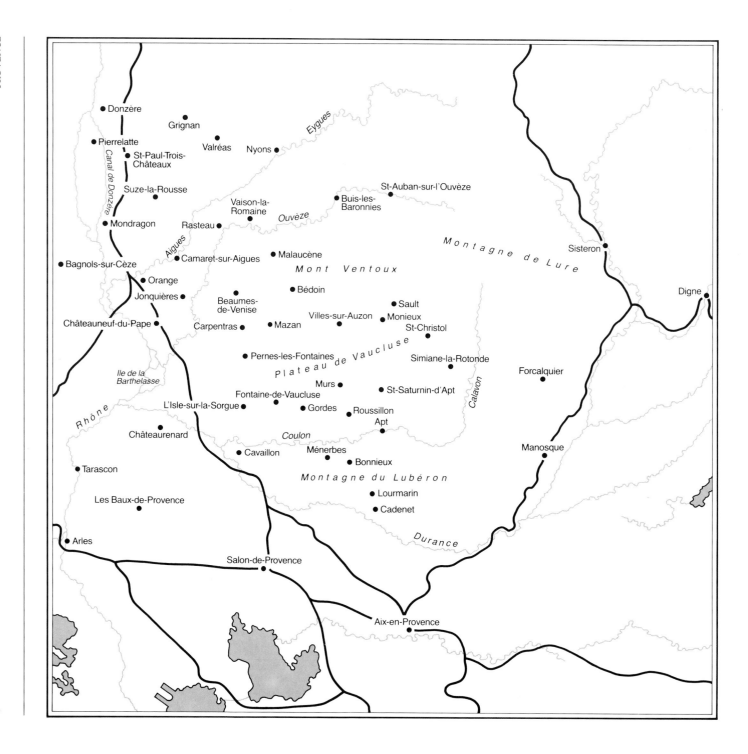

1
The Gateway to Provence

Donzère – Valréas – Nyons – Vaison-la-Romaine –
Carpentras – Gorges de la Nesque – Orange –
Châteauneuf-du-Pape – Fontaine-de-Vaucluse –
Apt – Montagne du Lubéron

The traditional belief that no olive trees will grow north of a line drawn roughly from Donzère through Nyons and across to Sisteron may not be entirely true, but it is a useful guide to the northern boundary of Provence. Most of the cultivable land in this particular area is in fact dominated by the vine rather than the olive. The vineyards are not neat and small-scale like those of Burgundy or even Beaujolais, but become ever larger as the alluvial valley of the Rhône widens to the south. This area is the Tricastin, named after one of the ancient peoples who lived here, and is the source of much cheap wine exported under regional labels. This wine is also used occasionally to fortify poor vintages of other wines which are rated more highly. But many individual wines from specific villages, such as those from Vacqueyras or Gigondas, are fine examples of their kind, often deep ruby-red in colour and spicy in flavour. Beaumes-de-Venise also produces one of the best dessert wines in all France, made from the muscat grape.

The cherry orchards are less extensive but equally striking. In spring dense, white blossom contrasts violently with the severely pruned vines, with the purple of small lavender plantations and with the pale yellows, oranges and greys of the soil. Buildings echo these colours and their roofs are customarily weighted down by large stones against the mistral. Even modern houses adopt this seemingly primitive but effective measure and the angle of many trees is a further reminder of the wind's force. In spring, before they are burned brown by the relentless heat of summer, the fields are bright with wild flowers. One in particular, a brilliantly blue hyacinth, is said to be deadly poisonous. And there is the light. Not as intense as it is further south, where reflection from the Mediterranean helps to produce a very special quality, it is none the less different from the light to be found only a hundred kilometres or so to the north. It is a presence, an integral part of the Provençal atmosphere of which no-one can remain unaware. Crossing over the Donzère-Sisteron line, therefore, you get a strong impression of having moved, quite suddenly, into a new environment. This is where Provence truly begins.

This northwestern corner of Provence is in the *départements* of the Drôme and the Vaucluse, the latter deriving its name from *vallées closes* (enclosed valleys). In all directions mountains block the horizon. Fifty kilometres away to the southeast lies the commanding presence of the Mont Ventoux. Rising to nearly 2000 metres, this is easily the bleakest and most impressive mountain in this part of France. Villages such as La Garde-Adhémar, or Mondragon and Mornas 15 kilometres further south, are planted on outcrops of

A soaring complex of Christian symbols at La Garde-Adhémar.

rock or strategically placed at vantage points. Many retain parts of their original fortifications, reminders that this was the northern and most vulnerable part of the frontier between France and Provence. Châteaux are also substantial monuments to a region that was once prosperous and powerful. Some, such as those at Suze-la-Rousse or Rochegude, resemble fortresses rather than country houses.

Within 20 kilometres to the east of Donzère, the Château de Grignan unexpectedly comes into view round a sharp bend in the road (N541). Medieval in origin, the château was substantially altered in the sixteenth century by Gaucher d'Adhémar and thereafter by his son the Marquis de Grignan, Louis XIV's principal representative in Provence. From certain angles it resembles the more flamboyant châteaux of the Loire valley and looks almost out of place. Its many noteworthy features include some fine

tapestries and pieces of furniture, but its most striking aspect is the south-facing terrace. On the roof of the chapel and largely sheltered from the mistral by the main body of the house, there are magnificent views from here, and on clear days it is possible to see into four different *départements*: Vaucluse, Ardèche, Drôme and Bouches-du-Rhône. The seventeenth-century writer, Madame de Sévigné, whose daughter married Grignan in 1669, much admired this terrace with its fine balustrade. In her letters she frequently praises the beauty and comfort of the château as well as the delights of Provençal food – roast pheasants stuffed with thyme or quails were favourites. She was less enthusiastic about the weather, however, which she often found cold and depressing: 'We are at the mercy of the winds . . . all the rivers are plagued by them and even the Rhône is powerless to resist. Our writing desks are frozen and we breathe only snow.' She visited her daughter on three occasions, died at the château and is buried in the family tomb.

Like several other villages in the region, Grignan has benefited very considerably from its historic buildings and associations. The massive shape of the château dominates the huddle of houses from the top of a large outcrop of rock. On the northern and eastern flanks the medieval buildings, often built of a pale, honey-coloured stone, and the cool, narrow streets have been vigorously restored. In its way the result is pleasing, though like the *vieux quartiers* at Vaison-la-Romaine, for example, this part of Grignan has not entirely avoided the modern trend for arts and crafts.

Less than 20 kilometres to the southwest is a small hilly area centred on Saint-Paul-Trois-Châteaux. This village lies on the Via Agrippa and, as in many other local villages and towns, the remains of a substantial Roman community have been discovered. Rather more curious, however, are the thirteenth-century frescoes in the church depicting scenes of cruelty and torment. One, for example, shows a Saracen prisoner wearing a

Suze-la-Rousse: an early reminder of Provence's former strength and elegance.

sheep's head and being led away (for execution?) by two Roman soldiers; another represents the Last Judgement with demons torturing various Church dignitaries. The abandoned village of Barry just to the south of Saint-Paul is also curious. Barry — a word which derives from the Provençal for rampart and is found throughout the region in the street name, rue du Barri — overlooks the Rhône and the plains of the Drôme. With its remains of a twelfth-century château it is another reminder of the fortified frontier, but today Barry is more notable for its view over the massive hydro-electric station of Donzère-Mondragon. Built between 1948 and 1952 by the Compagnie Nationale du Rhône, this was the second of its kind. In addition to providing electricity, this station also ensures control of the Rhône and adequate irrigation for the surrounding areas.

Since the late 1960s various military and nuclear centres have been developed here as well, with considerable consequences for what used to be essentially a relatively self-contained rural area. Some agricultural workers have left the land altogether, others combine farming with industrial work. The population has grown rapidly, especially with recruitment (largely from Paris) in the managerial class. New communities have developed, such as Pierrelatte or Bagnols-sur-Cèze further south, the latter claiming to have the youngest population of any town in France. Not surprisingly many local people, and especially the old, have remained suspicious and hostile. For them the Rhône has been deprived of its mystery and power. They are also convinced that the mistral is now much weaker than it once was as a result of this interference with nature, and that mists and poor weather have become more frequent.

To the east of Barry and Saint-Paul and before the mountainous areas flanked by the north face of the Ventoux fully assert themselves, is an area rich in variety and interest. Seen from a distance, Valréas sits

The former wash-house at Grignan.

Artistry in wood and stone at Saint-Paul-Trois-Châteaux.

enticingly on its low, round hill, and with its concentric structure is typical of a small medieval Provençal town. Although the town's original walls have mostly been replaced by a ring-road, parts of the medieval sector and of the two châteaux still remain. The Hôtel de Ville, once a splendid town house belonging to the Simiane family, some of whose members eventually became linked by marriage to the Grignans, should also be visited. The seventeenth-century proportions and decoration on the first floor (especially some wood-carving, plaster-work and painting) have been kept almost intact, and the library contains a fascinating collection of books and documents of regional interest. These are particularly important because Valréas has a unique position within an enclave of the Vaucluse, entirely surrounded by the department of the Drôme. For financial and political reasons the area was sold to the Papacy in

1317 and developed into an important legal centre. During the Wars of Religion the Baron des Adrets tried to seize it on several occasions, but was defeated by Catholic troops led by the Comte de Suze. The town remained an object of controversy and dispute until the late eighteenth century. It was reunited with the Drôme in 1791, but subsequently became part of the Vaucluse and has remained so ever since.

Before continuing further east to Nyons it is worth following the valley of the Pègue to the village of the same name overlooked by the southern flank of the Montagne de la Lance. Excavations here have unearthed abundant evidence of both Gallo-Roman and Greek communities, showing just how deeply these civilizations penetrated the interior of the country from the southern coast. If they then found it difficult to go any further, this is not surprising. The hills rise steeply from the gently undulating, fertile land between the Lez and the Eygues, reaching more than 800 metres in places. At Nyons the Montagne des Vaux ends abruptly in Le Trou de Pontias which, according to legend, marks the spot where the wind of the same name first appeared. Nyons had long suffered from drought and the local people appealed to the Archbishop of Arles to rid them of it. He agreed to look for a wind that would cool the village in summer and eventually found one on the coast near La Ciotat to the east of Marseille. He trapped it in a glove, returned to Nyons and hurled the glove against the rocks calling on God to assist him. At once the rock face split open and the Pontias began to blow. Today it ensures an exceptionally agreeable climate. Protected from the mistral as well, Nyons rarely experiences frost, and it is not unusual to find mimosas and pomegranate trees growing in private gardens. Olives are also widely cultivated, especially those of the finer quality whose fruit can be eaten (*olives de table*) rather than grown for oil. But in general in this area farming is made difficult by an increasingly mountainous terrain, and the

inhabitants of Nyons have been obliged to rely on their village's reputation as a health resort for much of their income.

To the east of the town the mountains sweep round in a majestic fold to form the long range of the Baronnies which marks the northern edge of Provence. It is possible to follow them from Nyons to Buis-les-Baronnies only on mountain tracks or by taking the *Grande Randonnée 9*. Access by road along the valley of the Ouvèze from Saint-Auban to the east or Vaison-la-Romaine to the west is much more tortuous, but this principal approach (D5) passes through countryside which begins to resemble that of the lower Alps. The hills rise steeply from the river valley and in spring the pines are often still brown after a hard winter or late frost. The trunks of young olive trees may be protected by cardboard or plastic sheeting and piles of neatly cut logs bear witness to a climate that can be severe.

This is splendid walking country, some of the best in Provence, though even the official paths demand care. For those equipped and willing the Col de Malpertuis just northwest of Buis, the Clue de Plaisians to the south, or the Montagne de Bluye are only some of the more interesting possibilities which could be attempted before trying Mont Ventoux. For the less adventurous, however, the road east from Saint-Auban and Buis (D546) provides a foretaste of what is to come towards Digne and Sisteron. Of the villages, Buis itself is a thriving community lying at the confluence of roads and river and protected on all sides by the hills. Like Entrechaux (whose name derives from *intercallis*, or crossing of the paths) some 15 kilometres to the southwest, it benefits from agriculture and tourism alike, and both have an air of prosperity about them. The whole area is also rich in history. Remains of prehistoric settlements have been discovered and the valley of the Ouvèze is riddled with grottos and caves. Two more recent buildings are also striking; the church at Pierrelongue on the road from Buis to Entrechaux, which is perched high on a narrow core of rock, and the tenth-century ruined château at Entrechaux.

Just to the north of Entrechaux the Ouvèze

Valréas, set elegantly amongst the trees of upper Provence.

Above **The foothills of the Baronnies.**

Right **The extraordinary perched chapel of Pierrelongue.**

meanders through a valley and down into the most important town of the area, Vaison-la-Romaine. Old prints of Vaison show virtually nothing of the Roman remains. Like those at Glanum (see p. 79) they were not discovered until early in the twentieth century, when scientific excavations were begun in 1907. Vasio, as the community was known, was clearly an impressive and sizeable settlement. Substantial private dwellings, public baths, shops, offices and religious buildings, many richly decorated with mosaic work and precious stones, are all clearly displayed. The grandest site of all is the open-air theatre, which is large enough to have seated 7000 spectators and has a perfect acoustic. Restored in the 1930s, it is used for concerts during the July festival. Vaison's Roman past permeates many other areas of the town apart from these official archaeological sites. The cathedral church and cloister of Notre-Dame-de-Nazareth, with its beautifully proportioned romanesque arches, visibly stands on what was probably a pagan temple. Its date of origin has long been a subject of academic dispute. Less grandiose but more intimate reminders of Roman life are some tiles in the town's museum, bearing imprints of a child's bare foot and dogs' paws. And many a garden wall has been constructed from stones which centuries ago may have been put to a different and more dignified use.

A sturdy Roman bridge links this part of Vaison with the later medieval *quartier*, topped by the ruins of its originally twelfth-century château on an outcrop of rock to the south. This part of the town, with its walls, two fortified doorways, remains of an episcopal palace and typical twisting streets, is rapidly becoming fashionable. Much of the restorative work is good, with some particularly fine doors and windows – though many of the once open drainage channels have been crudely filled with asphalt. Lintels occasionally bear dates, usually from the seventeenth and eighteenth centuries. Virtually free from traffic, this side of Vaison is attractive, though, as at Grignan, it has not entirely escaped the lure of the tourist industry. The views from the château ruins are splendid, both over the town as a whole and east towards the mountains.

South of Vaison lies the thickly wooded area of La Payre and beyond that, as the land rises, the small, jagged range of peaks known as the Dentelles de Montmirail, the very end of a fold running east-west in the Alpes du Sud. Their delicacy (*dentelles* means lace), especially when they are seen against the sun, is deceptive. Though neither extensive nor particularly high (734 metres), they have long provided testing climbs for mountaineers of all standards. From the western edge of these hills vineyards disappear into the distance, their monotony broken only by small patches of arable farming or cherry orchards.

By far the most attractive route is to follow the line of villages tucked in against the hills which stretch south from Vaison – Séguret, Sablet, Gigondas and Beaumes. Each has its individual charm. There are fine houses, Roman and medieval remains and grottos near Beaumes (whose name derives from both the Latin *balma* and the Provençal *baou*), and views either east to the Dentelles or west over the plain towards Orange. Walks in this area, mostly well indicated, are many and various. This is also one of the oldest – and most interesting – wine-producing regions of France. The local reds from the slopes of Gigondas or Vacqueyras, or the sweet, dessert muscats from Beaumes or Rasteau further north near Vaison, are vastly superior to most of the bulk wines produced in the lower part of the Rhône valley.

Vegetables and fruit from this whole region also have an immediate and highly organized outlet based on the market towns of Carpentras, Cavaillon and Châteaurenard. Between May and October between 150,000 and 200,000 tonnes of produce are sent throughout France and abroad. Two express trains per day, time-tabled to meet with rail, sea and air connections, ensure a continuous flow of goods which can command high prices, but are also delicate and perishable. Local rivalry is high. If Cavaillon is

The Dentelles de Montmirail seen from the vineyards west of Gigondas.

Sablet – just one of several delightful villages tucked in against the flanks of the hills south of Vaison, with the Dentelles in the distance.

renowned for its melons, Carpentras specializes in early strawberries. You can sometimes buy these, at a price, as early as April.

The biggest of these three towns, Carpentras, lies south of Beaumes on the route from Vaison and is today surrounded by a busy main road. Of the original walls erected in the fourteenth century by the Avignon popes, only one fortified gate remains, the Porte d'Orange. By comparison with the villages for which it is a natural focal point, Carpentras is a bustling, almost aggressive place. For reasons that are difficult to define, it gives the impression of having failed to blend its undeniable and considerable historical interest and attractiveness with the demands of the modern world. This is summed up for me in a way by the decaying west façade of the one-time cathedral of Saint-Siffrein,

which dates from the fifteenth century. Yet there is much to see and many of the buildings are now protected.

The most interesting and unusual of them all is the synagogue, which is the oldest in France. Although Jews were officially expelled from Provence early in the fourteenth century, the Avignon popes were reluctant to lose their financial skills. Consequently they were offered sanctuary in a number of local towns such as Carpentras, Cavaillon and Forcalquier, where communities have remained ever since. Though considerably restored in the eighteenth century, the synagogue at Carpentras retains much of its earlier beauty as well as tokens of an active Jewish life. The baths used in the ritual purification of young women before marriage can still be seen; so too can the ovens used to bake unleavened bread. And the whole building is rich with carving and decoration. Equally unique is the eighteenth-century Hôpital Notre-Dame-des-Grâces, with its original staircase and superb collection of glazed pots and mortars in what is now a pharmacy. In the Bibliothèque Inguimbertine are more than 200,000 volumes (including 4000 manuscripts), which constitute one of the richest libraries in the south of France outside the Méjanes at Aix-en-Provence. There is also an important art collection in the Musée Duplessis which, amongst others, contains works by Ingres, Vernet and Flandrin.

Another museum, the Musée Contadin, displays a range of bells, all of different tone and pitch, which are worn by goats, sheep and cattle as they are taken to graze on the higher grasslands in spring and brought down again in autumn. At those times of year when transhumance takes place, the sounds of the bells reverberate through the hills for many kilometres. Herdsmen are able to recognize their animals by the sound they make, and the sight of huge flocks moving across distant mountainsides or crowding through narrow village streets is impressive. In northern areas of the Vaucluse, or on the Plateau de Valensole to the east, this activity often has ritualistic Christo-pagan associations, while an interesting literary echo is to be found in Jean Giono's novel *Le Grand Troupeau*, based on World War 1. In this powerful book, to show how wrong and unnatural war is, the sheep are seen coming *down* from the cool of the mountains in summer, driven on by some kind of mad impulsion.

Whatever its atmosphere, Carpentras does have much to offer in its own right; it is also a convenient departure point for a number of substantial but self-contained and quite different excursions. The first, to the north and east, embraces the northern slopes of the Plateau de Vaucluse, the Plateau d'Albion, the Gorges de la Nesque and the Mont Ventoux. The second, much more limited in scope, is northwest to Orange and Châteauneuf-du-Pape. The third lies south through L'Isle-sur-la-Sorgue towards Cavaillon, and thence east along the narrowing valley in the direction of Apt, while the fourth takes you immediately south into the Lubéron hills. Together these excursions cover the rest of the department of Vaucluse and are a splendid illustration of its variety, complexity and mystery.

There are two possible routes over the fertile plains around Carpentras to the Plateau d'Albion, which lies some 600 or 700 metres higher. The first is southeast to Venasque, across the thickly wooded Plateau de Vaucluse and eventually to Sault and Saint-Christol.

Like Gordes immediately to the south across the plateau, but on a smaller scale, Venasque is a colourful village in an impressive site. Built on a spur of rock, it is tucked between two small but quite steep ranges of hills and has been extensively and intelligently restored. The village has notable Roman, medieval, seventeenth- and eighteenth-century parts, though the church of Notre-Dame is perhaps the most outstanding individual building. At the northern point of the spur and much restored in the eighteenth century, it stands on remains which have been dated to the sixth century. Its floor plan is in the relatively unusual shape of a Greek cross and it is adjoined by a baptistry, a large, vaulted building which supposedly originates from the seventh century. It is certainly the oldest baptistry in the Vaucluse and is thought by some to have been a temple devoted to Venus.

Conscious of its attractiveness, Venasque is re-

Cathedral wall at Cavaillon: intimations of mortality.

latively quiet for much of the period from autumn to early summer as though in preparation for the influx of tourists and semi-permanent residents. But it also benefits from a thriving agricultural industry, with cherries and truffles playing an important role. In May and June there is even a daily market devoted almost entirely to the sale of cherries. Each variety is carefully labelled, but these names will be quickly lost once they reach the shops.

The forest of Venasque to the east is best crossed through the Combe de Vaulongue and then over the Col du Puy de Griffon (D4). The main road continues south to Murs with its interesting stone wall (Le Mur de la Peste) on the north side. This was built in the eighteenth century as part of the village's attempt to keep bearers of the plague at bay – and its own inhabitants inside! But before you reach Murs a smaller road rising to over 800 metres cuts back

Above **Lavender plants at Aurel near Sault.**

Right **Spring yellow near Saint-Christol.**

through the forests of Bourrade, Saint-Lambert and Javon to the tiny hamlet of Saint-Jean. Saint-Christol can only be reached by road from here by going south to Saint-Saturnin-d'Apt or north to Sault, but it is possible to find more direct ways on foot. Indeed the best way to explore almost all this superb plateau is along various tracks, some of which, it has to be said, are often difficult to discover. Unexpected outcrops of rock, dramatic, plunging valleys, isolated farmsteads and occasional mills all contribute to the attractiveness of this area, for the most part thickly covered with pine, oak and beech. But by Saint-Christol both landscape and atmosphere have changed quite strikingly. The dark green of the Vaucluse plateau is now replaced by an almost treeless expanse stretching away to the foothills of the Lure mountains to the northeast and the Ventoux to the north. On clear days it is possible to see the snow-capped lower Alps quite easily.

This rather desolate area, the Plateau d'Albion, is really a geological depression between the uplands of the Ventoux and the Lure. Its chalky rock is riddled with grottos (*avens*), some of which, such as those of La Caladaire or Jean Nouveau, have been explored to depths of over 300 metres. Many of them can be visited. The chalk itself serves as an underground reservoir from which water passes beneath the Plateau de Vaucluse, reappearing 600 metres lower at the Fontaine-de-Vaucluse, which lies at the bottom of the plateau's western escarpment. This natural drainage system is so effective that the Plateau d'Albion appears almost desert-like at times. But cereal crops and potatoes are cultivated and there is also extensive grazing. Local income has received a very considerable boost, however, from the establishment of a nuclear missile base in the late 1960s. This lies just to the north of Saint-Christol and now employs well over 2000 people. This particular site was chosen because the Ministry of Defence considered that the *avens*

One of France's major nuclear stations is not far from here.

provided ready-made sites for silos, even though at the time there was a proposal to turn the plateau into a natural park. Over thirty buried silos now exist, and the whole camp, surrounded by an unwelcoming wire fence and warning notices, has what *Le Monde* once fittingly described as 'the atmosphere of a cemetery'.

Far less sinister, but with similarly defensive intentions, is the curious building which dominates the tiny semicircular village of Simiane-la-Rotonde, just 10 kilometres to the southeast of Saint-Christol in the department of Alpes-de-Haute-Provence. This building is basically a small keep with an accompanying chapel, and tradition suggests that it was designed by nobles from the Simiane family of Valréas, who are thought to have seen similar ones while on Crusades in the Holy Land. A rather more prosaic explanation is that its design has been copied from that of the kitchen quarters to be found in some of Provence's abbeys. Whatever the truth, this is a fascinating building which should not be missed, even though it is now sadly falling into disrepair. It has six panels on the outside and twice as many irregular ones on the inside, and the whole construction is topped by a lamp-house. As a look-out post it is perfect, and looking back towards the village from the south it is at once obvious that it would have been impossible to approach it unobserved.

Dramatic and varied as this route east from Carpentras is, it is less so than the more northern one dominated by the Gorges de la Nesque. This starts in a leisurely fashion through the attractive villages of Mazan and Villes-sur-Auzon. Both are pleasantly surrounded by woods, but Villes has the more spectacular site, lying at the foot of a range of hills which sweep round from the Mont Ventoux to the north. The histories of Mazan and Villes-sur-Auzon are violent and tormented. Both communities were pillaged and laid under siege by the Baron des Adrets in the sixteenth century and later suffered from various outbreaks of plague.

Mazan also has links with that most violent man of eighteenth-century French literature, the Marquis de Sade. One of the family's several châteaux was here

The church of Notre-Dame-de-Pareloup at Mazan.

authentic costumes, and this suggests that it will not be held regularly. The two notable local beliefs are associated with the Cimetière du Bon Remède to the northwest of the village and with Notre-Dame-de-Pareloup on the eastern edge, both of which seem to be integral to local folklore and may be connected with each other. The cemetery contains a collection of beautifully made Roman sarcophagi, worthy of comparison with those at Alyscamps in Arles, and locally believed to provide protection against vampires. It seems that they may have been effective, since another superstition holds that the now half-buried eleventh-century chapel of Notre-Dame was built to exorcise demons who came at night in the guise of wolves to unearth and devour corpses. This superstition is reflected in the chapel's name – Pareloup, literally 'against the wolf'. On a windy, midwinter night, or on a stormy afternoon in November when mists swirl around the summit of the Ventoux, it is difficult to suppress the feeling that a hostile presence is not far away.

Just east of Villes-sur-Auzon the road (D942) climbs quite steeply through the Combe de l'Hermitage before turning sharply south to join the Gorges de la Nesque. At first the road is curiously neat. Low evergreen hedges at the sides are trimmed as they might be in the centre of a prosperous suburb, seeming out of place at the entrance to an area of wild mountainous terrain. Apart from the Gorges du Verdon, these are without question the most spectacular in Provence. About 20 kilometres long (from Méthamis at the western end to Monieux at the eastern), they lie along the line of a massive fault, a zone of weakness which has been further eroded over the centuries by the River Nesque, now dry for many months of the year. In places the gorges plunge to depths of over 300 metres, and the whole area is thick with scrub and rocks, and riddled with caves. Sometimes the road appears to have been

and it has been restored and turned – ironically and perhaps out of contrition – into a rest home. Two hundred years ago it was the scene for productions of some of the Marquis' plays and as such is said to have been the site of the first ever Provençal festival. The château has been very substantially altered, but still contains fine original plaster-work. Mazan is also one of the foremost producers of gypsum in the world, and there are interesting tours of the local factories.

Three local traditions and beliefs connected with Mazan are particularly worth attention. The first is the Fête du Carri, based on the custom, going back to 1725, of a peasant who becomes lord of the village for a day (1 May). He rides through the streets in a special cart (the *carri*), drawn by fifty horses and followed by crowds of people in period dress representing all ranks of society. Abandoned for many years, this *fête* has now been revived, but there have proved to be considerable problems in organizing it and finding enough

Gorges de la Nesque. The road clings to the side of the cliff, often, as here, cutting through an overhang of rock.

chiselled out of the very face of the cliffs which continue above and sometimes overhang it. Tunnels and hairpin bends add to the drama and the vistas in either direction are superb.

Two thirds of the way along towards Monieux on the southern side is the Rocher du Cire. This huge concave rock rises to over 200 metres above the road, and is so called because of the wax deposited on it by millions of wild bees who have turned it into a massive hive. Local inhabitants say young people from Sault and Monieux used to hang from the top by long ropes and collect the honey until only very recently, though the practice seems to have been abandoned. Rather less dangerously the whole area is full of possibilities for long, testing walks, either south to the Plateau de Vaucluse or north to the Ventoux. The *Grande Randonnée 9*, for example, crosses the gorges just to the east of the Rocher du Cire and follows the fault line as it curves round by way of Monieux, passing only 5 kilometres west of Sault.

Like many mountainous areas in Provence, the Gorges de la Nesque convey an impression of peace and, especially in summer, they provide an opportunity to escape from the relentless heat of the sun. The Mont Ventoux, however, is different. It imposes its presence on the region round about in a way unlike any other mountain in Provence, except perhaps the Sainte Victoire to the east of Aix. A massive pyramid of rock, it is a mountain of infinite moods and atmosphere; it can be sinister, threatening or appealing, but rarely gentle. On stormy days it can be shrouded in cloud one moment and brilliantly clear the next. Snow-capped for at least six months of the year, from November to April or May, it will be burned dry by August, its 2000-metre summit a semi-desert of bleached stones and parched soil. And almost always the wind after which it is named (Ventoux means the windy one) gusts violently and disturbingly.

By contrast, the gentler lower slopes, especially those facing south, are well watered by springs and are rich in plant life of all kinds. The celebrated nineteenth-century Provençal botanist and entomologist, Jean-Henri Fabre (1823–1915), spent some time studying the plant life of the mountain and recorded how it changed with altitude. He noted, for example, that the sun-loving thyme found on the lower slopes is gradually replaced by the hardier saxifrage usually found in much colder northern parts, and he observed a tiny yellow poppy native to the tundra of Greenland growing near the summit. Bees feeding on this varied plant life produce honey of many different flavours and in spring the sides of the mountain are dotted with hives brought up by nearby villagers. Some of the herbs found on the mountain, like the *fustet* or the *genestelle*, are also associated with the rather more mysterious realms of natural Provençal medicine, in which interest is growing rapidly. The variety of trees is equally striking. Descriptions of the mountain before the mid nineteenth century refer to it as being virtually a stony desert, but reforestation was begun in earnest around 1860. Now, it is notable for its plantations of oaks, olives, beech, cedars and pines, the tree species varying according to altitude.

In 1336 Petrarch and his brother climbed the Ventoux from Malaucène at its western end. This was a much more strenuous excursion than it would be today when most people go to the top of the mountain by car. The views from the mountain, back west across the Rhône or east to the Alps, will not have changed all that much, but the Ventoux itself has. The summit is now occupied by a chapel (La Sainte-Croix), an observatory, a radar station, television masts, ski-lifts and a hotel, each in its own way emblematic of different values of modern society. Despite such intrusions, the Ventoux still remains something of a challenge and a law unto itself. The Romans – whose historians make no mention of it – presumably considered the technical difficulties of colonizing this mountainous area not worth solving. But they may also have been wary. Just as ancient historians believed the Camargue to be the gateway to the underworld, so it is tempting to suppose that they may have seen the Ventoux as the site of a different, mysterious culture

Mont Ventoux: snow-capped even in late spring.

Left **Autumnal evening sun to the east of the Mont Ventoux.**

Above **Brantes on the north side of the Mont Ventoux. The sound of the church bells reverberates for kilometres through the valley.**

ready and able to dispel unwelcome visitors at all times.

From Sault the summit road crosses the high point of the mountain at the aptly named Col des Tempêtes, where a number of paths lead off across the steeper northern flank towards the Montagne de Bluye and the valley of the Toulourenc. From here onwards to any of the small villages to the east of Vaison is relatively straightforward. The road itself winds down into Malaucène after only 25 kilometres, passing the Rochers des Rans from which there is a splendid view northwest across Beaumont-du-Ventoux towards Vaison. Just outside the village is an area known as Le Groseau, worth visiting for its warm spring and the remains of a papal summer palace built by Pope Clement V. As a whole, Malaucène has several buildings bearing evidence of its prosperous past – a massive fortified fourteenth-century church, an eighteenth-century hospital and some fine town houses.

In earlier times, this prosperity was partly due to papal favour, but today it is more reliably based on farming in the fertile basin of the Groseau river, which is protected on all sides by wooded hills. Fruit and vegetables are particularly profitable here, but local honey, wine and cheese are also much in demand. In addition, Malaucène has the reputation of being the place where potatoes were first grown in Provence. Much of the old village, dominated by a fifteenth-century clock tower and the remains of a château, is now being vigorously restored and it seems likely that Malaucène will become a fashionable town, conveniently situated as it is on the main road between Vaison and Carpentras.

On the route south back to Carpentras two detours are recommended. The first is to the pretty, densely-packed village of Le Barroux just off the main road to the west. This is dominated by its superb château, an interesting mix of medieval fortification and Renaissance elegance. Over the years it has suffered extensively from fire, pillaging and general decay, but it is now largely restored. Like the Château de Lourmarin (see p. 61) on the southern edge of the Lubéron, it is a cultural centre which particularly welcomes foreign students of Provençal history and customs. The second detour takes in Bédoin to the southeast, a village full of delightful medieval remains (especially the church of Sainte-Madeleine) and houses built from local ochre-coloured stone. On market days Bédoin becomes a near solid mass of stalls selling everything from pottery to lavender. This is a local village at its best – busy, colourful, prosperous and self-assured.

The name of the one remaining medieval gate at Carpentras – La Porte d'Orange – is a reminder that Orange is not far away. The road linking the two towns runs northwest across the alluvial plain of the river Ouvèze, which joins the Rhône just north of Avignon. This whole area, like the plain of La Petite Crau to the west of Cavaillon (see p. 79), supports intensive market gardening and fruit-farming, and is covered by a lattice-work of irrigation channels and wind-breaks of cypress trees. It is flat, relatively uninteresting but prosperous, as communities such as those of Sarrians or Jonquières indicate. Another feature is the number of large houses and châteaux (like those north of Aix) built over the centuries as country retreats for the wealthy families of Avignon and Orange. Many now give the impression of being half-abandoned, but two still in prime condition are worth visiting: the Château de Tourreau on the outskirts of Sarrians and the Château de Beauregard at Jonquières.

The Château de Tourreau is a delightful classical folly built in the mid eighteenth century by the Avignon architect Esprit Brun. The central portion is extended on both sides by two wings, gently curving round to form a quarter circle embracing the main courtyard, and the whole building looks out over lawns shaded by century-old plane trees. Beauregard is older and quite different in character. Built in the mid sixteenth century, its square floor plan and

Still life at Bédoin.

rounded corner towers capped by *poivrières* are typically Provençal. The outbuildings are covered by *tuiles romaines* and the central courtyard contains an elaborate – but ill-kept – maze of dwarf box hedges. The château has remained in the hands of the same family since it was built but, unlike Tourreau, is not open to the public.

From Jonquières the most interesting approach to Orange is by the minor road which goes directly north to Camaret-sur-Aigues, a village which is notable for the fact that it has won the national championship for the rather dangerous hybrid sport of *moto-ball*, a form of polo on motor cycles, several times! If for no other reason though, it should be visited for the superbly restored ornamental campanile which adorns the main town gate in the original walls, arguably one of the finest of its kind in Provence. Like a number of other villages in the area, Camaret is a thriving community with prosperity based on fruit- and vegetable-farming and the increasingly prevalent vine.

This whole fertile area between the Rhône and the Dentelles de Montmirail bears traces of various Celtic and Ligurian settlements. Despite its fierce resistance to the Roman army, the principal site, Arausio, was eventually colonized in 36 BC by veterans from Augustus' second legion. Sheltered from the mistral by hills to the north and with relatively good communications along the Aigues and the Rhône, the settlement quickly developed in importance. The range and efficiency of the bureaucratic activities of the Romans stationed here is well shown by their survey records of areas as far afield as Nyons and Montélimar. These were carved in marble slabs and can be seen today in the town museum at Orange.

Many of the Roman remains at Orange were quarried for building material in the seventeenth century, but examples of the town's early splendour still remain, in particular the Arc de Triomphe and the theatre. The triumphal arch was, of course, a tribute to

the Romans' power and is richly decorated with scenes of military and naval exploits and of naked Gauls captured by Roman soldiers. It is a magnificent monument, but unfortunately stands at the edge of the town on that main and most unpleasant arterial road, the N7, a modern Via Agrippa. The theatre too is a monument to Roman supremacy and the one here is in a far better state of preservation than that at Vaison. Thought to have once seated over 12,000 people, it is a fascinating and very complete illustration of the intricacies of a Roman theatre. The stage, wings, passages for spectators and storage rooms can still all be seen, but the most impressive feature is undoubtedly the famous backdrop. This enormous wall, 103 metres long and 36 metres high, is covered with niches, pillars and blocks to ensure a perfect acoustic, and was described by Louis XIV as the finest in all his kingdom. What he would have done with its central feature is a matter of interesting speculation. A massive statue of Augustus, nearly 4 metres tall, towers above the stage, his arm raised in triumph over a Gaul cowering at his feet.

From the time of the Roman settlement Orange was to have a distinguished but disturbed history. A bishopric was established in the fourth century and a university in the Middle Ages, though this was suppressed at the time of the Revolution. Orange was sacked by the Visigoths in the fifth century, ravaged by disease on many occasions and extensively damaged by fire during the Wars of Religion. In the late sixteenth century it was linked through marriage to the Dutch noble house of Orange-Nassau (hence its present name), and remained independent for a hundred years until it was claimed by Louis XIV. French possession was formally recognized in 1713 by the Treaty of Utrecht.

Although Orange's real splendour comes from its Roman heritage, there are also some fine and interesting buildings from later years. The ruins of the château built by the Orange-Nassau family lie on the hill of Saint Eutrope to the south behind the theatre, a point from which there are spectacular views of the whole town. The restored twelfth-century church of

---

The twelfth-century church of Sainte-Madeleine at Bédoin.

Above **Imperial salute: the statue of Augustus towering above the stage in the theatre at Orange.**

Left **The triumphal arch at Orange.**

Notre-Dame-de-Nazareth, built on the ruins of a pagan temple to Diana, and a number of town houses in the place des Frères Mounet are especially worth a visit.

Modern-day Orange is almost permanently busy, especially from mid April to mid October when there is a daily market. Even though it is now bypassed by the *autoroute*, traffic jams are the rule rather than the exception. In many respects the town is overshadowed by Avignon, but it gives the impression of working busily at making the most of its natural advantages.

Also, like Salon to the south, it has benefited economically from the establishment of an important military airbase, in this case at Caritat. Its people are proud of its historical inheritance and it is a town that should not be bypassed.

A similar independence of spirit also marks the small, internationally famous village of Châteauneuf-du-Pape to the south, with its celebrated vineyards. Although only 10 kilometres from Orange, the change in scenery from the area further north to this block of undulating land between the *autoroute*, the Rhône and its tributary the Meyne could hardly be more marked. Fertile irrigated fields have been replaced by a mass of carefully tended vines growing on what frequently looks like little more than a layer of rubble. Yet these cream- and rust-tinted stones are essential. They act as storage heaters, absorbing the warmth of the sun and reflecting it back to the vines. In July and August they can remain warm to the touch long after sunset.

There are records of wine being made in this region from the twelfth century, but it was really only with Pope John XXII, who had built his famous château here between 1318 and 1333, that Châteauneuf-du-Pape became well known. Today many of the estates which produce the famous wine are still quite small, family concerns. Others have grown and some, like those of the Châteaux de Fortia or de la Nerte, produce labelled wine of international reputation. With few exceptions, however, the old style Châteauneuf wine, which used to be left to mature in oak barrels for five years before being bottled, has disappeared.

Yet even with modern methods of vinification the wine remains distinctive. Officially it may be made from a mixture of as many as thirteen different varieties of grape. Most growers use only seven or eight, but the result can still be a complex dark, inky wine which at its best will keep easily for up to twenty years. If modern-day sales figures indicate its current popularity, Pope John had also enjoyed it in 1324 when he celebrated the marriage of his great-niece. The meal to which it was an accompaniment almost defies the imagination; it included 55 sheep, 690 chickens, 580 partridges, 270 rabbits, 50 pigeons, 40 plovers, 37 ducks, 8 pigs and 4 boars. The amount of wine consumed is not recorded. . . .

In 1562 the château where these celebrations took place was destroyed by Protestant troops led by Montbrun and most of what remained was subsequently blown up nearly four centuries later by the Germans. Yet the ruins still convey some idea of the splendour of the original. From the hill on which they stand it is possible to see across the Rhône into the Ardèche, east to the Ventoux and south over the islands of Oiselet and Barthelasse to Avignon. Châteauneuf is in fact rather like an enclave within Provence and its pride, community spirit and independence are best experienced in the village itself at the time of the *vendange*, or grape harvest. Then, to quote one authority, 'the streets of the village swarm with activity. . . . Open doors reveal newly washed barrels, lengths of rubber piping and churning presses. From even the quietest alleyways drifts a smell of fermenting must.'

Highly fertile and intensively cultivated, the area to the south and west of Carpentras is very similar to the one which extends towards Orange. Channels and streams criss-cross the land, draining into small rivers like the Sorgues, Nesque or Velléron, which in turn feed the Rhône to the west or the Durance to the south. From the east the lower slopes of the Plateau de Vaucluse, dotted with quarries, push up to the road running from Pernes-les-Fontaines to L'Isle-sur-la-Sorgue.

With its 32 fountains, Pernes is aptly named. A spring, discovered in the mid eighteenth century, has provided a major source of drinking water ever since and the fountains, now all carefully signposted, are the town's principal attraction. Some, like the Fontaine du Cormoran topped by an effigy of the bird with a fish in its beak, are listed monuments. Others have legends associated with them. Water from the Fontaine de la Lune for example, can, as its name suggests, send people mad. The Fontaine du Gigot is so called on account of its resemblance to a leg of lamb. Pernes lies on the Nesque and this too is an attractive feature. With its beautifully tended quays, it provides a

Above **The remains of Pope John XXII's palace at Châteauneuf-du-Pape.**

Right **Gloriously fresh, Pernes-les-Fontaines is one of the most attractive of Provence's inland villages.**

natural focal point for this prosperous little town which ranked higher in local administrative and political importance than Carpentras until the early fourteenth century. Much of the old town is still surrounded by parts of the original walls which were begun at that time (like those at Avignon), much restored two hundred years later but extensively damaged in the mid nineteenth century. Some of the gates are impressive, such as St Gilles with its large square tower, or Notre Dame with its fortifications and drawbridge.

These walls and towers enclose a neat, compact collection of well-proportioned secular and religious buildings (including the remains of the eleventh-

century château), frequently built from a rich honey-coloured stone. Many repay attention, but none more so than the Tour Ferrande just inside one of the other original gates, the Porte Villeneuve. Dating from the thirteenth century, the rooms in the tower were once decorated from floor to ceiling with frescoes. Unfortunately only those in the upper room have survived and even these are quite badly worn. Although perhaps of no great artistic merit, they do offer an interesting record of certain aspects of medieval aristocratic life. Some are religious in inspiration, others depict battle scenes, and many are of tournaments and jousting ceremonies which may owe more to medieval romances than to reality. These frescoes are amongst the oldest in France, and bear comparison with the rather finer work in the Chambre du Cerf in the Palais des Papes at Avignon. Today Perne's activities are rather more modest than those depicted. Market gardening is the major source of income: strawberries are a local speciality, while the asparagus market is the most important of the region.

Only a few kilometres to the southwest of Pernes, on a hill which was once surrounded by marshes between the villages of Velléron and Le Thor, is the Grotte de Thouzon. This is well over 200 metres long and contains a fine collection of stalactites. Le Thor is also worth visiting for the church of Notre-Dame-du-Lac, a beautiful example of late thirteenth-century Provençal romanesque architecture. The buttresses, the roof boss depicting the Lamb of God, and the hexagonal apse are only some of the attractive details which make this one of the finest churches of its style in the region.

Somewhat confusingly the Sorgue river which runs through Le Thor is also found at Velléron, and local people will insist on calling another half dozen tributaries by the same name. Rising from the Fontaine de Vaucluse just over 10 kilometres to the east, the Sorgue splits into five streams at L'Isle-sur-la-Sorgue, a community of growing importance which is about twice the size of Pernes. The old town is entirely surrounded by water and is known as the Venice of Provence. Gondolas appropriately appear during the summer months, though in fact it is more likely that the town's nickname derives originally from the old province of Venayssin. Mill wheels, now attractively preserved, are reminders of the source of energy that once supported thriving industries in weaving, leather goods and dying. The continuing importance of fishing is enshrined in the names of many streets, such as Anguille (eel), Truite (trout) and Ecrevisse (crayfish).

L'Isle-sur-la-Sorgue lies only a few kilometres from the narrow entrances to the valleys of the Durance and the Coulon, the latter running east to Apt between the Plateau de Vaucluse and the Lubéron. When the mistral from the north is funnelled into these valleys, L'Isle-sur-la-Sorgue is subject to particularly violent winds. One telling piece of evidence is the fact that the windows on the north side of the church of Notre-Dame-des-Anges were regularly blown in and have been walled up since 1666. The town is centred on this church with its Italianate belfry and baroque exterior, and on market days it rises above a sea of colourful market stalls and animated cafés. The eighteenth-century Hôtel Dieu with its imposing entrance and stairway is another notable building. Like the Hôpital Notre-Dame-des-Grâces at Carpentras, it contains an impressive range of pharmacy pots.

L'Isle-sur-la-Sorgue's principal claim to fame today, however – and the source of much of its income – is its proximity to the Fontaine de Vaucluse, one of the most extraordinary natural phenomena in the whole of France. Now attracting over one million visitors a year, the Fontaine is one of the biggest tourist centres in the country. It can be quickly and directly reached from L'Isle, but a more attractive route goes by way of the tiny *village perché* of Saumane just to the north, which was given to the de Sade family by Pope Clement V. The château here has been much restored, but is worth visiting for its eighteenth-century *salon*, Renaissance staircase and vast, rambling cellars. There is also a group of pine trees permanently bent at an alarming angle by the force of the mistral.

An impressive gorge leads to the Fontaine from Saumane. A deep freshwater pool lying at a height of nearly 250 metres is backed by a sweep of steep cliffs across which it is possible to have guided walks (though these are not for the faint-hearted). The spring that feeds the pool is thought to be the natural outlet for a vast reservoir which, according to some theories, underlies the Plateau de Valensole and parts of the Lure, as well as the Plateau de Vaucluse. Legend also links this natural reservoir with the water system in the area of the Sainte Victoire to the east of Aix-en-Provence. On average the spring produces 2.5 million cubic metres of water per day, always at a constant temperature of 12° to 13°C. At times of heavy rain, this amount rises to nearly 200 cubic metres *per second*, or nearly eight times as much; and as the pressure from the underground spring increases, so the emerald green colour of the water becomes richer.

The pool is overlooked by the Vache d'Or, a rock whose shape vaguely resembles that of a cow. Local tradition holds that a vast store of gold is buried beneath the rock, but that any attempts to discover it are greeted by a loud bellowing. This story is obviously linked to those concerning the golden goat at Glanum, Les Baux and elsewhere. It may also have become confused with that of the Couloubre or *couleuvre* (a word widely and indiscriminately used for snake or lizard), which is said to have terrified the local population for years in the sixth century. According to one version, St Véran, the patron saint of shepherds, overcame the beast and led it away by an iron chain to the Lubéron where it smashed its way through the mountain, thereby creating the Gorges de Lourmarin across the Lubéron. (Mignard's painting of this episode can be seen in the cathedral at Cavaillon.) Another version claims that the Couloubre devastated the region around Cavaillon in its rage and frustration before flying away to the Alps and settling in the community which subsequently became known as Saint-Véran. A small black and gold lizard found around Fontaine today is thought to be the Couloubre's descendant, and is said to be unable to grow any bigger because it lost its ancestor in this way! The Couloubre story is itself a variant of the many dragon legends in Provence, such as the one about Tarascon (see p. 87).

In addition to its spring and legendary creatures, Fontaine-de-Vaucluse is also celebrated for the fact that the poet Petrarch left Avignon and spent a considerable amount of time there between 1337 and 1353. He had met Laure de Noves ten years earlier and came to Fontaine to ponder and write about her beauty in a series of immaculately formed and celebrated sonnets. No-one knows precisely where he stayed, though at least four houses in the village have claimed to be the *maison de Petrarch*. One, a so-called museum, is distinctly disappointing.

South of Fontaine-de-Vaucluse a long ridge of the plateau runs down towards the western end of the Lubéron and the narrow entrance to the valley of the Coulon. Here the pretty villages of Lagnes and Cabrières, with its cedar trees and plague wall, can be reached easily by car. A good walk for the more energetic is to cut up due north from Fontaine along the *Grande Randonnée 6*, which crosses the peak of Mourre de la Belle Etoile to Pouraque and then turns abruptly southeast towards Gordes. About 5 kilometres north of the village the path drops down into the valley of the Sénancole and passes the remote Abbaye de Sénanque.

Founded in the twelfth century, this abbey is linked with those at Silvacane and Le Thoronet in a group known as the 'three sisters of Provence'. Sénanque was sold to the State in 1790; but was re-occupied by monks of the Cistercian order by the mid nineteenth century. The monks finally left in 1969 to join a community on the Ile de Lérins off the coast at Cannes and the abbey is now a cultural and study centre specializing in Saharan affairs and medieval studies; it can be reached by a narrow road from Gordes. Its superb, austere buildings have been well preserved, the acoustic in the abbey church is excellent and the presence of dozens of masons' marks cut into the stone somehow compresses its eight hundred years of existence. But the site is oppressive. The abbey is dwarfed by the steep sides of the valley, and the surrounding oak trees (one of which is said to be six hundred years old) create an atmosphere of grimness. In summer the valley is a suntrap, the air heavy with

the scent of wild herbs and the heat accentuating the grey of the stone and the violet of the lavender. In winter it can be bitterly cold, with the wind howling down the Vallon de Ferrière from the north.

Austerity and bleakness are also features of the curious *village noir* only 4 kilometres away, just outside Gordes. This is a community of dry-stone dwellings (*bories*), most of which resemble something like a cross between an igloo and a beehive. They are also found locally elsewhere, and are often now no more than heaps of stones. They are thought by some to be ancient primitive dwellings which were once used by semi-nomadic shepherds; others are of the opinion that they were used by people trying to escape from plague epidemics. Those near Gordes probably date from no earlier than the seventeenth century and have certainly been inhabited during the last hundred years.

The site is now preserved as a museum and several of the *bories* contain nineteenth-century tools and furniture. An exhibition, which includes photographs, gives a good idea of how the community once existed, with people earning a basic living from spinning and leather-work. The extent of the site, which is completely walled, shows that the community was quite large and must indeed have once resembled a complete village. Some privately-owned *bories* have been plastered and modernized; the result is not unattractive, but it is a far cry from the original dwelling which, despite its apparently crude structure, is robust and, except in the windiest weather, surprisingly draught-proof.

A rough track from the *village noir* approaches Gordes from the west, giving dramatic views of one of Provence's most spectacular *villages perchés*. Built on a natural defensive site overlooking the plains to the south and east, it is easy to appreciate why Gordes was important in Roman times. Its invulnerability con-

tinued. During the Wars of Religion Adrets' attempts to take it were all unsuccessful, and it was an important centre of the Resistance movement in World War 2. Inside the village the houses seem to be virtually piled on top of one another, ready at a moment's notice to slip down the hillside.

Dominating the whole site is the fourteenth-century château which, like so many in the area, once belonged to the Simiane family. It was substantially altered in the sixteenth century and is now a study centre and museum inspired by the Hungarian mathematician and designer Vasarely. His work, which can be seen on a much greater scale at the Fondation Vasarely in Aix-en-Provence, demonstrates the search for forms in which he said 'art joins science to [. . .] satisfy both our sensitivity and our present knowledge'. The results, full of shifting perspectives and illusion, are disturbing and fascinating.

South and east of Gordes, between the Lubéron and the Plateau de Vaucluse, lies a fertile plain which rises gently as it approaches Apt. Many of the slopes in this valley are planted with vines producing some fine, underrated Côtes du Lubéron wine. But above all this is orchard country. The region is famous for its jams and preserved fruit and in spring fields of pink and white blossom herald a soft fruit harvest that is usually amongst the best in France. Less welcome, perhaps, are signs of extensive residential development, and changes in local legislation are likely to lead to a proliferation of modern houses, which may not blend easily into this attractive countryside. Property for sale in the hamlets and villages has been much sought after for over a decade. The tiny community of Croagnes, directly east of Gordes, for example, which is barely more than a handful of farm buildings, is now almost entirely owned by English, Swiss, Belgians and French from the north. Yet communities such as Croagnes would otherwise decay, and at least partly as a result of outsiders acquiring property the local church is now used for services once a month. What further changes the planned increases in population will bring remain to be seen, however.

Between Gordes and Croagnes an attractive road

Abbaye de Sénanque: the most isolated of Provence's 'three sisters'.

51

runs north by way of Joucas – yet another one-time property of the Simiane family – and through a narrow valley to Lioux. Suddenly the countryside becomes much more rugged. The Combe de Lioux and the Falaise de la Madeleine, a wall of rock over 100 metres high and more than a kilometre long, dramatically fringe the plateau at this point. From here you can continue north along the D943 and the D96 through the gorge of La Sigalière and the Forêt de Javon to join the eastern end of the Gorges de la Nesque at Monieux. In a large clearing about 10 kilometres from Lioux is the local sixteenth-century château, which is in a fine state of repair. Its rounded towers, *poivrières* and stone-mullioned windows are all complete. Inside is a stone spiral staircase which bears comparison with the one in Lourmarin (see p. 61). The massive fireplace in the *salle des gardes* (guard room) is also original, as is much of the furniture, notably some leather armchairs and a large dresser. Bordering the main path to an ornamental pond in the gardens is a series of twelve statues representing the months of the year.

Beyond the Château de Javon the countryside continues to rise towards the Plateau d'Albion – in places reaching over 1000 metres. The road from Sault (D943) follows the contours along the edge of the plateau as it winds southwards to Saint-Saturnin-d'Apt, known locally as Saint-Sat. Famous for its château (now ruined) and three windmills, Saint-Saturnin has a history which dates from neolithic times. A rich hoard of bones and primitive utensils indicating very substantial settlements was found here and is now in the natural history museums at Lyon and Paris. Today, there is still a substantial number of medieval and eighteenth-century buildings, and the whole village is seen to advantage from the high point of the château, reached by a steep, rough path through the ruined precincts. On the way you pass the reservoir which is the village's water

One of Saint-Saturnin's windmills on the edge of the Plateau de Vaucluse.

The houses in Gordes appear to be piled on top of one another ready to slide down into the valley at any moment.

supply. If the dam wall were to break there would be catastrophic destruction, but local people remain phlegmatically unconcerned.

Saint-Saturnin is also the home of one of Provence's most famous mystics, Rosette Tamisier. Born in 1818 and miraculously cured of what seems to have been some kind of open abcess, she entered religious orders. In 1836 she is supposed to have planted a cabbage upside down in the convent garden which grew so enormously overnight that the whole community of nuns was fed for a day. During the next few years she claimed to have visions and experience stigmata, while in 1850 she said she had witnessed blood issuing from Christ's wounds in a painting of the *Descent from the Cross* in a chapel in Saint-Saturnin. Accused of trickery, she called on local doctors and judges to support her. After witnessing the same phenomenon themselves, they did so publicly, but doubts and

53

persecution continued. A year later Rosette was tried and imprisoned, at which point these miraculous events stopped abruptly. She was released and appears to have fled to Villeneuve-lès-Avignon. All further records of her life have either been destroyed or lost; so too, somewhat conveniently, has the painting.

Down in the valley just 10 kilometres away is Apt itself, once an island in the Coulon or, as it is known here, the Calavon river. This still skirts the town to the north, but on the southern side its course is now a main boulevard. The walls of the *lycée*, however, still retain their old mooring rings. Apt was an important centre for the Romans. Traces of a theatre and of thermal baths have been discovered, and the original grid pattern of the streets can be seen quite clearly on any town plan. Sacked by the barbarians in the fifth century, it was for long virtually uninhabited and only began to re-emerge as a commercial centre during the Middle Ages.

Today the prosperous central rue des Marchands is a pedestrian area, still spanned by an attractive sixteenth-century clock tower and belfry. A stone's throw away is the cathedral of Notre-Dame-de-l'Assomption, arguably the finest of Apt's historic buildings. Dating from the eleventh century, it is built on the foundations of an eighth-century Carolingian church. A series of sarcophagi in what was the original crypt predate the first church by three hundred years. The cathedral also contains a rich collection of paintings and relics, including those of St Anne, mother of the Virgin Mary, which are said to have been discovered under the floor of the chancel at Easter 776 on the occasion of a visit by the Emperor Charlemagne.

Like Saint-Christol nearly 30 kilometres to the north, Apt has both grown and benefited economically from the development of the nuclear centre on the Plateau d'Albion. Many of the personnel live here and the old town is overlooked by a growing number of high-rise blocks, clearly built for convenience and efficiency rather than attractiveness. Yet the old agricultural traditions and activities of this prosperous town are still very much alive – the Whit Sunday fête with its colourful procession of horses and carts, or the Fête de Sainte Anne when grapes are offered to the saint, are two well-patronized seasonal events. Apt is also the principal market for much local fruit and jam (including an especially delicious cherry). In fact Madame de Sévigné's description of Apt as 'a jam cauldron' remains just as true now as it was three centuries ago. And one particularly attractive side-effect of fruit farming in this area is the super-abundance of butterflies, including some of the rarest species in France.

Colour of a different kind derives from ochre quarries, the most famous of which is the one at Roussillon, half-way between Apt and Gordes. Here seventeen different shades of soil were once worked, varying from a pale yellow to a deep violet, all of which clash dramatically with the dark green of the surrounding pines. Since any extension of work at this quarry would have endangered the very foundations of the village, ochre is no longer extracted here. It is rain rather than human hands which has carved and smoothed the soil over the years into the fantastic shapes seen in the abandoned quarry known as the Vallée des Fées. At Rustrel, northeast of Apt, columns of red ochre capped by clay look rather like giant mushrooms. In both Rustrel and Roussillon, as elsewhere, ochre quarrying – like bauxite mining around Brignoles – is dying rapidly. In the early eighteenth century large quantities used to be taken by mule to Marseille for export or for use by local industry. Today, faced with competition from chemical dyes, demand and production have fallen by 80 per cent.

Whatever the fate of the industry, however, one legend will remain. The area around Roussillon once belonged to Raymond d'Avignon. Frequently absent on hunting expeditions, he would leave his wife Sirmonde to be entertained by his page and troubador, Guillaume de Cabestang. The couple fell in love and, on discovering this, Raymond had the young man killed and his heart fed to his wife at a banquet. She

The ochre cliffs at Roussillon.

threw herself off a cliff in despair and a spring issued from the spot where she fell. The legend also has it that her blood stained the entire region ochre-red.

Finally, protecting the southern boundary of the Vaucluse and overlooking the great sweep of the Durance from Cavaillon in the west to Manosque in the east are the Lubéron hills, designated since 1977 as a protected nature reserve. Much of this region is thickly wooded and is rich in plant life. In October and November the oaks and beech trees can rival parts of the forests of the Var to the east (see Chapter 5) in their magnificent blaze of autumnal colours. Although less exposed than much of the Plateau de Vaucluse or parts of the hills around the Ventoux to the north, the Lubéron is none the less a challenge. Scored with deep valleys and caves and with many of the roads closed to traffic, it is ideally explored on foot. However, for those who prefer to progress on four wheels, a road crosses the mountain from Apt to Lourmarin on the route to Cadenet and thence to Aix. This road conveniently divides the Lubéron into two sections. The eastern one is less populated, though the villages at the foot of its northern slopes are attractive and many have points of interest. Near the tiny community of Auribeau, for example, evidence of neolithic tribes has been discovered; Bioux boasts some fine grottos and stalactites; and Sivergues is said by one source to derive its name from a fifth-century convent known as the 'Six Virgins'. These three, together with Castellet, are set on promontories overlooking the fertile valley of the Calavon and its tributaries and are backed by the steep wooded face of the Sommet du Mourre Nègre. But it is the western and more rugged section of the range which is both better known and more interesting. This is dominated by the imposing Massif des Cèdres, best visited on winter evenings, when the wind howls from the north through the giant trees, recreating an eerie atmosphere of mystery, magic and violence.

Beyond the Massif to the south the escarpment

An enchanting corner at Saignon, south of Apt.

plunges over 500 metres within no more than 3 or 4 kilometres. In parts nearly impenetrable, this area is a reminder of the Lubéron's bloody and violent past, barely equalled by that of any other part of Provence. For centuries the whole range provided a place of refuge for persecuted groups – druids, hermits, those classed as religious heretics, and eventually the Protestants. Without question, one of the worst incidents in Provençal history concerned the *vaudois*, followers of Pierre de Vaux or Petrus Valdo – Peter of the valleys or possibly Peter the sorcerer. He had had the Bible translated into Provençal and as a result was excommunicated by the Church in 1179. Those who practised his basic, fundamentalist beliefs were likewise outlawed and fled to various mountainous areas in France – to Piédmont, the Alps and the Dauphiné. By the fourteenth century they had found their way to Provence and in 1332 were declared to be heretics by the Avignon popes. Persecution began on an ever-increasing scale. By the middle of the next century Vaudois and Protestants had joined forces and Innocent VIII organized what was literally a witch-hunt, resulting in hundreds of burnings and imprisonments.

Despite the intercession of Louis XII these persecutions continued and the Catholic Church appointed a Dominican Jean de Roma to act as its inquisitor. His methods were uncompromisingly brutal, and even though Vaudois and Protestants withstood his attacks, the operation was too advanced to be halted. Local disasters – floods, frosts, poor harvests, disease – were blamed on them and in 1539 François I ordered that they should be punished. Despite a brief reprieve, an army of over 4000 troops led by Jean Maynier systematically devastated the area in 1545. Hundreds were massacred; over twenty villages were totally destroyed and in some cases had their names erased from the map. Mérindol-le-Vieux on the south side of the Lubéron is today still only a heap of rubble.

Some of those persecuted were initially successful in escaping to the higher and wilder parts of the mountains, but many were forced out of hiding by

Above **The Château de Lourmarin in the southern foothills of the Lubéron.**

Right **Mist and autumnal beauty at Bonnieux.**

starvation or when Maynier set fire to the hillsides. Of those imprisoned, nearly a thousand were burned to death or were sent to the galleys. It was only two hundred years later, after the Revolution, that the Vaudois would be allowed, like the Protestants, to practise their beliefs freely. Even the Marquis de Sade, whose château was at Lacoste on the northern edge of the Lubéron and who did not himself shirk descriptions of the most appalling atrocities and sufferings, complained bitterly of the deep scars left by the whole affair.

Only Lourmarin, the capital of the Lubéron on its very southern edge, substantially escaped this devastation, and saw the establishment of a Protestant community. Today Lourmarin is neat, prosperous and busy and property is much in demand. There are some fine town houses with beautifully arched doorways and windows, and a selection of pigeon-lofts (including one with a curious double roof). The château just outside the village, which can be visited, was restored in 1920 by Laurent Vibert and turned into a study centre for talented young artists, musicians and writers. Its massive stone spiral staircase, an ornamental fireplace on the first floor, and a series of fourteenth-century wooden balconies overlooking a courtyard on its eastern side are particularly impressive. Throughout the year residents from the centre and hikers who walk the *Grande Randonnée 97*, which passes through the village, ensure a lively, colourful atmosphere. It is also a place of modern literary pilgrimage. Henri Bosco (1888–1976), a writer of highly charged, almost supernatural Provençal novels, is buried here; so too is Albert Camus (1913–60). Camus' house on the western side of the village is a museum and more or less permanent exhibition centre. His grave is covered with wild rosemary.

Beyond Lourmarin and back in the Lubéron itself,

Ménerbes: the one-time impregnability of the Lubéron villages is soon appreciated. Cars are not allowed into the village.

the violent events of five centuries ago are now buried deep in the past, the only witnesses the village stones and paving slabs. Many houses are now being restored and are much in demand by Aixois and those in search of a *résidence secondaire*. But the special atmosphere of this area can still be sensed, particularly at night when the lights of the villages on the northern slopes remind one of isolated encampments huddled in upon themselves for protection. In some ways such separateness is still a feature of village life. Although communication between Bonnieux, Lacoste, Ménerbes and Oppède-le-Vieux is quite straightforward – the youth of these villages soon prove that in their noisy, supercharged cars – each is proudly different and repays leisurely examination.

These very real links with a turbulent past are paralleled by the continuing presence of a less tangible struggle in the Lubéron. Long before the religious disputes the area was rich in magic; dwellings, even relatively primitive ones like the *bories*, would be built with a piece of glass or vitrified stone in the walls to act as a talisman to ward off evil spirits. (This practice resembles that of placing a bull's horn on the roofs of the herdsmen's *mas* in the Camargue.) A thistle is still nailed to the gateway of a sheep enclosure on the higher slopes for the same reason. And the shepherd himself has long been considered by generations of peasants in the Lubéron to be a direct link with ancient Celtic tribes and in particular with their priests. He is thought by some to possess knowledge of good and evil, of the forces of nature, of the medicinal properties of plants and herbs and, above all, to have an intuitive power which enables him to perceive and ward off harmful presences.

It is, of course, easy to romanticize. As around the Ventoux, on the Plateau de Vaucluse or that of Valensole further east, such beliefs are probably based on the vestiges of a more prosaic confrontation between plain (and town) dwellers on the one hand, and hill people on the other. Yet these are matters which even today should not be dismissed too readily or cynically. If the Ventoux and Vaucluse have magic and mystery about them, so does the Lubéron.

2
Marseille and its Hinterland

Marseille – Salon – Les Baux – Saint-Rémy –
Avignon – Tarascon – Arles – Camargue –
Saintes-Maries-de-la-Mer

To arrive in Provence down the Rhône valley from the north is a gradual and subtle experience, to do so by way of Marseille is dramatic – even brash. Between the limestone ranges of the Estaque to the west and the Massif de Marseilleveyre to the southeast, and backed by the Chaîne de l'Etoile, Marseille occupies an impressive position. Until the German invasion and occupation in 1943, it proved for centuries to be well-nigh impregnable. Second only to Paris in size and importance, linked internationally by rail, sea and air, Marseille has a gloss and an air of self-confidence and importance normally associated with capital cities. It is above all – as it has been for 2500 years – a trading centre relying heavily on the sea. Even though the forest of masts in the Vieux Port may today point more to private wealth and pleasure than to commercial activities, it is not difficult to imagine how this part of the town, the first to be settled, must have appeared in earlier times.

Marseille has romantic origins. In approximately 600 BC Greek traders from the eastern Mediterranean arrived and were welcomed by the local tribe, the Salyens (a name which probably indicates their trade in salt). The chief's daughter Gyptis took the Greek leader Protis in marriage and a community was established known as Massilia or Massalia. Its growth was rapid; it came to rival Carthage as a Mediterranean

port and was of obvious strategic importance. Julius Caesar captured it in 49 BC when the town threatened to side with Pompey in his challenge for supreme power within the Roman Empire. In subsequent centuries it withstood attacks from pirates and the Saracens, and in the sixteenth century François I fortified the Ile d'If. The castle he built was subsequently made famous by the nineteenth-century writer Alexandre Dumas in *The Count of Monte Cristo*, the story about Edmond Dantès, the man in the iron mask. In common with other ports Marseille also suffered from diseases brought from distant shores. Its population was decimated at fairly regular intervals, especially during the last great plague in Provence in 1720 when some 50,000 people died.

Whatever adversity it has had to face, however, the spirit of Marseille has never been broken. For centuries it adopted positions at variance with the political climate of the rest of Provence. Louis XIV, no less, was obliged to visit the town in 1660 when he ordered the construction of two forts – Saint Nicolas and Saint Jean – to remind the people of his authority. And even today, when it has long been a bastion of the political left, Marseille has a reputation for awkwardness and for wielding an influence in affairs that is not entirely devoid of self-interest.

Individually the Marseillais are considered sharp-minded, resourceful, cunning and not always as generous and as affable as those immortalized by Marcel Pagnol in his novels and plays. Evelyn Waugh once wrote of them: 'They all tried to swindle me, mostly with complete success.' It is no secret that the much publicized fish market is seen at its flamboyant best during the height of the tourist season. More muted, just as authentic and more interesting are the early-morning fruit and vegetable markets. Peasants from kilometres around come to these now in battered vans, when only sixty years ago they came by horse and cart. The night-time manoeuvrings of the ships and massive container lorries in the industrial port areas are equally fascinating and a reminder of the sheer volume of trade conducted here.

Remains from Marseille's most distant past have been discovered on a number of sites, especially to the north of the Vieux Port. These are now housed in various museums, of which the Musée Borély has the most impressive collection. But the city as it is now is predominantly as it has developed since the early nineteenth century. Areas like the Canebière, the original hemp (*chanvre*) market where rope makers once congregated (and now a focus for seekers of a different kind of hemp), have grown into important axes and focal points. Individual buildings like the Palais Longchamp (and its gardens), the cathedral of Sainte-Marie-Majeure or Palais de Justice testify to prosperity under the Second Empire in the mid nineteenth century. So too do the many fine façades of what are now apartment blocks, often with shops on the ground floor. The church of Notre-Dame-de-la-Garde, known locally as Bonne-Mère, watches over the port from its dramatic vantage point more than 160 metres above sea-level. Remarkable for its flamboyant appearance, pilgrims flock here on 15 August. More recent years have produced Corbusier's residential development, the Cité Radieuse, and the new railway station – both examples of that curious French capacity for inventiveness that unfortunately often goes hand in hand with considerable disregard for people and their environment.

The French capacity for indifference draws atten-

Above **The Italianate front of the cathedral of Sainte-Marie-Majeure in Marseille.**

Right **The approach to France's biggest and most important port.**

tion to another more worrying aspect of Marseille. While the famous monumental staircase leading up to the Gare Saint-Charles may have long been a romantic meeting-place for the widely travelled, it is now also one for alcoholics, drug-addicts, the unemployed and the homeless. Like many a city of its size, Marseille has social problems which are now only too apparent. These are particularly severe in a few central areas almost entirely populated by North Africans and described by Michel Tournier in his novel *La Goutte d'Or* as 'a network of alleys dominated by the smell of curry, incense and urine'. In these the limits of tolerance have been stretched sometimes to breaking-point and there is, regrettably, an almost permanent sense of tension and latent hostility. There could be no

Above **Bulls in the fountain in front of the Palais Longchamp: a reminder that the Camargue is not far away.**

Right **Second Empire splendour: the Palais Longchamp.**

starker contrast than that between the near slum conditions of these inner-city *quartiers* and the expensive villas on the *corniche* to the east, or the *résidences secondaires* in the picturesque and carefully preserved fishing villages at the foot of the Estaque to the west. Nowhere else in Provence have problems of this kind reached such proportions, and they give Marseille a disturbing atmosphere.

In both size and character, therefore, Marseille is unique in Provence; focused on the sea, it gives relatively little indication of the kind of country which lies 50 or 100 kilometres inland. It is not difficult to find villagers on the Plateau de Valensole or even in the nearer Lubéron hills who have never been to Marseille and sometimes *vice versa*. And even more locally there is a sharp polarization between those who gravitate towards Marseille and those who prefer the more elegant atmosphere and smaller scale of Aix.

With the motorway system as developed as it is in this part of France, there is no problem about finding your way out of Marseille to explore the immediate hinterland. The road northwest to Salon is initially dramatic. The steep face of the Vitrolles mountains to the right is covered in scrub and pine trees, the splashes of red rock and soil a reminder that bauxite mining is a local industry. To the left is the massive Etang de Berre, dotted with oil tankers and lined with refineries. At night the burning jets of waste gas form a silent, eerie firework display. Thereafter the road becomes less interesting, though it is worth making a detour along the northern edge of the Etang by way of Saint-Chamas (prehistoric caves) and Miramas, where the old Roman and medieval village is gradually being resurrected as a much sought after location for *résidences secondaires*.

Salon-de-Provence itself is best known to French people today as the home of the national military flying school. Since its establishment in 1936 this has provided a regular source of income to a community

which was at its most fashionable before the Revolution and which would otherwise probably have drifted slowly into insignificance. As its name suggests, Salon was once on an important trading route for salt, the *route de sel*, and has long been recognized as the 'capital' of the olive-oil refining area. It is also ideally situated for a variety of excursions, whether to local sites such as the extraordinary collection of prehistoric caves, the Grottes de Calès at Lamanon to the north, or further afield to places such as Avignon and Aix.

Aware of this potential, Salon has used – and is still using – its relative wealth to make itself even more attractive. The central medieval part of the town has been turned into a pedestrian precinct full of cafés and fashionable shops. Several of these sell local arts and crafts, health foods and herbs, the last a reminder of the fact that Nostradamus (1503–66) lived here four hundred years ago. This great astrologer, who was to become a favourite of Catherine de Medici, made his reputation on the basis of his cosmetic powders and love potions, and also as a result of his success in finding an antidote for the great plague of Aix in 1546.

For all its efforts and undoubted attractiveness, however, Salon appears slightly artificial and self-conscious, showing signs of aping, if not yet rivalling, the still growing and very expensive conurbation of Aix to the east. Leaving the town in the opposite direction by the N113 can be a shock. Flanked at first by plane trees, which have been so carefully pollarded over the years that even in winter you have the impression of driving through a tunnel, you suddenly emerge into an enormous sky-scape with the road disappearing into the distance in a dead straight line for nearly 40 kilometres, until it reaches Saint-Martin-de-Crau.

This must be one of the most anonymous and disagreeable stretches of major road in Provence, matched only perhaps by the N7 north of Aix. (And the area just to the south of Saint-Martin itself has the doubtful distinction of being the municipal tip for Marseille, receiving two train loads of refuse each day!) Water towers are much in evidence and occasional

---

The church of Notre-Dame-de-la-Garde watches over the Vieux Port in Marseille.

Above **Château la Barben, east of Pélissanne.**

Right **Château de l'Empéri, which now houses the local art and history museum at Salon.**

signposts point unconvincingly down tracks to tiny villages and *mas*, but all is hidden behind screens of cypress trees and bamboo. These wind-breaks are essential, for the wind, sometimes at gale force, bears down from the north and sweeps on across the vast plain of La Crau, a reminder of how large the delta of the Durance once was. Legend has it that this was the battleground where Hercules, with the assistance of Jupiter, overcame the despotic giants Albion and Bergion. The stones which the god threw down from the heavens still cover the plain. With the exception of the lake of Entressen to the north, popular with bird watchers and people fond of water-sports, this is mostly a disturbing, inhospitable place. Exploration on foot or by bicycle is not undertaken lightly. Mistral described it as a 'graveyard for millions of stones'.

As is so often the case, however, the unpleasantness is soon forgotten, for there are compensations. Only 15 kilometres or so away to the north are the Alpilles (or little Alps), where the novelist Alphonse Daudet's hero Tartarin came from Tarascon to train for his assault on Mont Blanc. Smaller in scale than the Ventoux or Lubéron ranges, the Alpilles are in some ways similar to the Massif de la Sainte Baume (see pp. 119–20), especially as it is seen from the south. Standing like irregular fortifications across the skyline, the limestone of which they are composed is so bare that their jagged peaks can appear snow-covered even in summer.

Villages such as Aureille, Eyguières, Mouriès and Maussane which lie right at their foot are all worth a visit. These peasant communities take advantage of a passing tourist trade during the summer months, but they are essentially private, their air of freshness and quiet prosperity a marked contrast to the increasingly savage landscape which is more typical of parts of northern Provence. In each case their freshness is due to ever-present water, as indicated by Eyguière's original name, Castrum de Aquaria. Draining down from the Alpilles in surprising quantities even at the height of the driest summer, and syphoned from the Canal du Midi, water has been channelled over the centuries to form an extensive irrigation system of immeasurable value to those who draw their living from the soil.

The importance of water in this area can also be traced in a curious mix of pagan and Christian symbols. On the outskirts of Fontvieille, for example, just 10 kilometres west of Maussane, are the remains of a Roman stone altar bearing the carving of an oyster shell. This was no doubt intended in honour of Venus and as a symbol of the region's fertility. It is said that pilgrims on their way to the shrine of St James (St Jacques) at Compostela in the late Middle Ages saw a symbol of their spiritual quest in this '*autel de la Coquille*'. It is likely though that the link between James (originally a fisherman and often distinguished by a scallop shell) and Venus had already been made. Whatever the truth, the shell symbol is found widely in this part of Provence – in primitive rock carvings and, rather unexpectedly, on a capital in the cloisters of the abbey of Montmajour. It is no coincidence that the church at Mouriès is dedicated to St Jacques.

It is possible to cross the Alpilles by a number of routes from Mouriès. All wind up towards the hills through large, immaculately tended plantations of dark olive and almond trees, oaks and occasional vineyards. The soil, though less coarse and stony than in the Crau, is none the less difficult to work, but occasional and surprising areas of surface water and noisy irrigation channels are reminders of the source of the region's prosperity. In winter these south-facing slopes are bleak, and olive-harvesting around Christmas and the New Year can be a bitter experience; in the summer there is little shade for the worker or traveller alike and the prudent stay indoors. Isolated farms and *domaines*, rarely visible from the road, are shrouded in trees, seeking protection from both wind and sun. Despite evidence of modern equipment for the production of olive oil or wine, these places give the impression of having changed little in the last hundred years or more.

Perhaps because it is more intimate, this area seems

The Alpilles.

more welcoming than the remoter parts of the Plateau d'Albion or the Ventoux mountains. It is certainly well worth making the effort to visit it as the 10-kilometre *route des vins* (D78) from Le Destet to Maussane soon reveals. Fires have taken their toll of some of the vegetation, but the scenery is spectacular and the people, in spite of their constant grumbles about the difficulties involved, are proud of the way they have come to terms with the conditions around them. They respond warmly to interested enquiries and will talk of the subtleties of different kinds of olive oil and enthuse, with justification, about their '*petits vins*' in a way that is refreshing by comparison with the take-it-or-leave-it attitude of many of their compatriots to the north, such as those in the Rhône wine areas or in Burgundy.

At the western end of the Alpilles on their southern face is Les Baux, the extraordinary and probably most famous of Provence's *villages perchés*, though not the most picturesque. At first sight it appears to have been carved directly out of the rock (its name comes from the Provençal word for rock, *baou*) and parts of some buildings, like the church of Saint-Vincent or those in the tiny rue du Trencat, were indeed formed in this way. But most impressive of all are the labyrinthine remains of the fortress – crumbling towers, pigeon lofts, cellars, chapels and living quarters – a reminder of the once flourishing community of the comtes des Baux, who first settled here in the tenth century, after the Romans had departed. Described by Mistral in his *Calandal* as a 'race of eagles', they were a proud and powerful people who claimed to have been descended from the Visigoths and before that from Balthazar, one of the three wise men. Their crest is based on his emblem of the holy star, though it also belongs, interestingly enough, to the gypsies who spread through much of southern Europe from the east in the early Middle Ages.

Virtually impregnable in their fortress, the counts acquired a reputation for cruelty and barbaric behaviour. Supposedly they took a sadistic delight in hurling their prisoners from the top of the castle walls to the rocks hundreds of metres below. At the same time they were not simply a violent, uncultured people. Links through marriage to the noble families of Anjou, as well as those of Avellino and Andria in Italy, ensured that for several centuries their castle enjoyed a courtly brilliance envied by many and celebrated by the troubadours. But it was not to last. Absorbed into Provence as a whole by the end of the fifteenth century and beset by religious strife, the community of Les Baux – like its independent spirit – was gradually destroyed. First Louis XI and later Louis XIII, who had endured enough civil disturbance during his reign, had much of the castle and the fortifications destroyed. Many of the inhabitants of the village were dispersed, although not without compensation.

For a long time thereafter Les Baux was virtually dead. Not much more than a hundred years ago both Dumas and Mérimée reported finding only a handful of beggars here. Today it is different. With its expensive restaurants and souvenir shops, and a tourist centre and exhibition explaining that bauxite was first discovered here, it is best avoided, especially in daytime during the summer. Rose Macaulay even considered it vulgar. But at night or in winter, when it can be exposed to the bitterly cold mistral from the north, it assumes a quite different character, a fact recognized by Jean Cocteau who chose the village as the location for his dream-like film *Le Testament d'Orphée*. On such occasions, it is possible fully to appreciate the isolated nature of the village and to imagine life there as it was four or five centuries before, and even earlier. At Christmas too the ancient Christo-pagan ceremony of the shepherds' offering is celebrated at midnight – as it is elsewhere in Provence – in an atmosphere that is somehow not of the present day, even though seats are expensive and have to be booked well in advance! During the mass shepherds and shepherdesses, bearing fruit and gifts as a sign of fertility, accompany a cart containing a lamb in an ornate cage. The chief shepherd carries the lamb to the

Les Baux: few villages are more spectacular – few more popular.

altar and offers it to the infant Jesus. At the moment of the elevation of the host the lamb's tail is roughly pulled three times in order to make it bleat in worship. Sacrifice is not far away. . . .

Such echoes from history, tradition and superstition continue beyond Les Baux as the road (D27) climbs up over the crest of the Alpilles and plunges tortuously down towards Saint-Rémy through the Val d'Enfer. Here a mixture of natural erosion and quarrying has created a chaotic landscape said to have inspired Dante (who stayed at Arles and visited Les Baux) in his depiction of the nine circles of Hell in the *Inferno*. Today some of the underground quarries can still be visited; one, known as La Cathédrale d'Images, is now an exhibition centre. Others are blocked by iron doors, but some are open. Inside the huge caverns resemble enormous warehouses, their walls scored by the hewing of massive blocks of stone. Graffiti commemorating the visits of thousands unfortunately deface many of the lower surfaces of the most accessible, but there are some which are relatively untouched. These can be explored with care; so too can natural grottos like the Trau di Fado, the Fairies' Cave, and the lair of the witch Tavèn, all of them featuring passages, underground wells, stalagmites and church-like caves, and all gloomy and frequented by bats, known locally as the flies of hell.

Said to stretch for kilometres, these grottos were once inhabited, like the prehistoric caves at Lamanon or those to the west at Cordes, a reminder of the very distant origins of the Provençal people. Legend also has it that they are still occupied today by the Chèvre d'Or, a fabulous goat. This animal guards the treasure hidden in the Tavèn lair by Abdel Rhaman, the Saracen leader defeated in battle by Charles Martel in the mid eighth century. Like the dragon of Tarascon, the goat – *La Cabro d'or* in Provençal – has a permanent place in the bestiary of the region and is found in many places, sometimes taking the form of a cow (as at Fontaine-de-Vaucluse) or a ram. Some see the origin of

such legends in pagan worship; others, including Mistral, suggest they may have Satanic overtones. Whatever the explanation, the Chèvre d'Or has an assured place in Provençal folklore.

Beyond the Val d'Enfer and at the bottom of the northern slopes of the Alpilles lie Saint-Rémy and the remains of the ancient city of Glanum. Both town and country change markedly in character. The mystery and harshness of Les Baux seem a world away from the altogether more leisured atmosphere of Saint-Rémy, while the peaks give way to the fertile plain of the Petite Crau which stretches north to Avignon and the valley of the Durance. Saint-Rémy lies half-way between the Rhône and the Durance, at the meeting point of the routes from Avignon to Arles and Tarascon to Cavaillon, and was for long an important town. It is said to owe its name to the saint who, visiting the region around the year 500, exorcized a young girl possessed of the devil. She died, but he brought her back to life and her father, in gratitude, presented him with the land on which the town now stands.

Still bearing signs of its Roman civilization, Saint-Rémy, like Salon or Tarascon, is notable too for some fine examples of building from later periods. The twelfth-century church and cloisters of the former monastery of Saint-Paul lie on the south side of the town, and there are some splendid sixteenth-century houses whose elegant façades bear witness to the town's wealth during the Renaissance. And while it may not share Salon's bustle and self-awareness, Saint-Rémy can claim a different, cultural richness of its own. Nostradamus, who spent most of his life in Salon, and Frédéric Mistral were both born here, the first in 1503, the second in 1830. But most celebrated of all perhaps was Vincent Van Gogh, who came here from Arles in May 1889 as an inmate of the asylum which had been established earlier in the century in the monastery of Saint-Paul. Though only in the form of reproductions, the monastery now shows paintings which bear witness to the artist's disturbed state of mind. He had been abandoned by Gauguin who decided to return to Paris after only two months in

Tormented rocks near Les Baux.

what he called the 'stunted and parched countryside' of Provence.

During his stay at Saint-Paul Van Gogh produced about 150 paintings, including the famous series of olive trees. The best known of these is *La Promenade du soir* with its olives and cypresses, its mix of blues and blacks, its luminous night sky and the pair of faceless, fleeing peasants in the foreground. Although he suffered from bouts of violent insanity during some of the time he spent at Saint-Paul, Van Gogh also had periods of complete lucidity, and his response to the colours of the surrounding countryside – 'it reminds you of Delacroix', he once wrote to his brother Theo – was amazingly acute. He was passionate about encouraging others to go to Saint-Paul in order to share his response to the light and colours, and he actually tried to have his quarters turned into a studio. Looking towards the Alpilles it is not difficult to understand his enthusiasm. His pictures, like Cézanne's, capture that special quality of the Provençal atmosphere which was only surpassed for Gauguin in South America and Martinique.

As Van Gogh gazed south through the olive groves, pines and cypresses, he would have seen two striking Roman monuments. The first, a mausoleum, is one of the best preserved in France and was built to honour the memory of the Emperor Augustus' two grandsons, Caïus and Lucius Caesar. (It is also said today to be yet another of the places inhabited by the Chèvre d'Or!) The second is a triumphal arch, less well preserved, commemorating the fall of Marseille to the Romans in about 50 BC. But Van Gogh would not have seen anything else which might have indicated the presence of a town long designated on old maps of the region as Glanum.

The remains of a settlement were not uncovered until after World War I. For at least 1500 years these had lain beneath the alluvial deposits washed down from the Alpilles. Glanum is a mystery. Since excavations have gone on in earnest, some evidence of a neolithic community has been discovered, but the first substantial settlement was almost certainly Greek. The people involved may have been merchants from Marseille, and the community existed for several hundred years. Eventually the town was overrun by tribes from the east in about 100 BC, but was then resurrected by the Romans before being sacked once again during the Germanic invasions of the third century. With a prime site on the important Via Aurelia, the route between Italy and Spain, Glanum must have been flourishing, elegant and wealthy.

Augustus spent some considerable time here, and monuments to various members of his family, in addition to his grandsons, can be seen on what is today one of France's most important archaeological sites. The remains are in an excellent state of preservation and include temples, palaces, more humble dwellings, a complex water system, mosaics and some votive tablets to Hercules (known to the Roman soldiers as 'Hercules the drinker'), together with a life-size statue of him with his club. In all they bear favourable comparison with the Roman remains at Vaison.

North from Glanum and Saint-Rémy the triangular plain of La Petite Crau brings an abrupt change in both atmosphere and landscape. Bordered to the south by the Alpilles, to the west by the Rhône and to the east by the Durance, much of this area was under water in the Middle Ages. Today a complex system of canals, channels, ditches and sluices has turned what was once swamp and marsh into an intensively cultivated area specializing in fruit and vegetables. Superficially, however, like the larger area after which it is named, La Petite Crau seems to hold few temptations, and most travellers tend to cling to the road running through Saint-Rémy which will take them west to Tarascon or east to Cavaillon. And for many more, as they hurtle north or south on the Autoroute du Soleil, the only observable feature of note is the impressive site of Orgon, where the ruined castle and chapel of Notre-Dame-de-Beauregard tower above the Durance and the motorway.

Monuments to Roman glory in the reign of Augustus at Glanum.

But this small, relatively unexplored area deserves to be better known. Most of the villages and small towns have some element of historic or architectural interest. Noves, Graveson and Barbentane still have fourteenth-century gateways and sections of their original walls. The churches are squat, solid, fortified buildings with stone roofs; their belfries, once used as look-out points, are topped by spires whose ribs are decorated with a protruding, tooth-like motif. Streets are narrow and twisting, and a labyrinth of interconnecting cellars still runs beneath many of the houses. To the north Châteaurenard is built on one of the few points of high ground and has splendid views over the valley of the Durance. Only the two towers remain of the original château, which was built in the fifteenth century by the counts of Provence and destroyed during the Revolution, 'twin horns on the forehead of a hill' as Mistral called them. And dotted across the whole area are *mas* and small châteaux, many of them remote, often partly derelict and rarely showing signs of life.

In many respects this region is either dependent on or overshadowed by Avignon and Cavaillon. Yet, almost as if in defiance, it retains its own peculiar atmosphere of self-sufficiency and mystery. Traditions are strong. In the abbey of Saint-Michel-de-Frigolet in the hills of La Montagnette to the west, for example, there is a Christmas mass not unlike the one at Les Baux (see p. 74). The feast of St Eloi, normally held in most of Provence on 15 August, is celebrated throughout this region with much splendour on 25 June. Statues of various saints and of the Black Virgin are still used in several churches in ceremonies to invoke changes in the weather.

Such ceremonies seem to be almost as much pagan as they are Christian. At Maillane, for example, the black effigy of Notre-Dame-de-Bételen (i.e. Bethlehem) traditionally has the power to bring rain or to protect against disease, especially cholera which killed off

Chapel at Eygalières near Saint-Rémy, traditionally flanked by cypress trees.

nearly 500 people in the town in the mid nineteenth century. The same church also has a statue of the Sicilian virgin martyr St Agathe, who offers protection against storms and fire. (Legend tells us that her terrible sufferings at the hand of the Roman Quincien caused the creation of Mount Etna.) At Graveson, St Anthime has similar powers: he can bring rain, ward off disease, ease childbirth and protect children. In his memoirs Mistral describes the procession which used to take place on 27 April, Anthime's feast day:

When the rain was late in coming, the faithful of Graveson, chanting their litanies and followed by a crowd of people all with sacks over their heads, would carry the statue of St Anthime – bearded, mitred, with staring eyes and highly coloured – to the church at Saint-Michel-de-Frigolet. There, during the whole day, their food spread all over the grass, people would wait for the rain and get steadily drunk on the local wine.

If prayers remained unanswered the statue was dipped three times into a local ditch. And if it rained for too long, the inhabitants of Graveson simply changed saints and called on St Aureille to bring the wind! In a different context altogether, Laure, so rapturously worshipped by Petrarch in his sonnets, is said to have been born at Noves.

To the north, less than 5 kilometres from the Durance and overlooking the Rhône, is Avignon. Approached from the south the outskirts of the town, like those around Arles, are hardly attractive, though the remains of the Abbaye Saint-Ruf are worth a visit. St Ruf is said to have been the son of Simon of Cyrene who helped Christ carry his cross, and is reputed to have been the first to bring Christianity to this region. The abbey itself probably dates from the ninth century. But apart from this relatively minor distraction there is no reason to linger in the suburbs. Soon the walls of the medieval city – albeit much restored in the nineteenth century by the architect Viollet-le-Duc, whose work can be seen on an equally grand scale at Carcassonne in the Languedoc – rise up as impressively as they must have done 500 years ago, even though the moats and ditches have long been filled in.

Musical griffin on the wall of the National Conservatorium of Music and Dance at Avignon.

The name Avignon is said to derive from the Celtic word *avenio*, meaning 'town at the edge of a river', or 'town of the violent wind'. Either is appropriate. The most striking views of the city are from the north, from Villeneuve-lès-Avignon or from the Ile de la Barthelasse, particularly if it is seen on a blustery winter day when the river is stirring and grey, and the town appears unwelcoming and impregnable. But the mood here, as in so many places in Provence, changes quickly. The stone of the walls responds to the sun, varying from near white to what the nineteenth-century novelist Stendhal described in his *Mémoires d'un touriste* as 'the colour of dried leaves'.

Like its name, the origins of Avignon are obscure. In 1960 a stone carved in human form and thought to be a fertility symbol was discovered inside the town walls in the garden of the Rocher des Doms. Similar in kind to others found in the surrounding region, especially near Orgon to the southeast, it was thought to provide evidence of tribal settlements on a fairly large scale, dating back to well before the birth of Christ. Certainly there was once a fishermen's colony here and later the Greeks established a trading post. Thereafter the site was developed by the Romans – remains of civic buildings and some tombs have been discovered – though Avignon was never as important as Arles or Aix. Like Glanum it suffered from a number of barbarian raids, at the hands of the Saracens and, less directly, at the time of the Albigensian wars in the early thirteenth century.

Less than seventy years later, at a time when the politics of Western Europe were in a state of turmoil, the King of France, Philip the Bold, had, under some pressure from Rome, ceded Avignon to the Papacy. Clement V, insecure in an Italy wracked by war, settled in Avignon early in the next century in 1309 and was followed in quick succession by six other popes. Much of Avignon as it now is, albeit much restored, is owed to these popes. The medieval chronicler Froissart, when he came upon the town, described it somewhat extravagantly as 'the finest and strongest in the world and easiest to defend'. Centuries later, Stendhal was impressed by its beauty and colour and likened it to an Italian city, while his contemporary Prosper Mérimée, best known for his short stories, records in his *Notes de voyages* that 'I thought I had left France and found myself in a Spanish town'.

Clement VI's additions to the papal palace of his predecessor, Benedict XII, must be the principal reason for such reactions. The first palace is a cold, austere dwelling of Cistercian inspiration which has led the modern novelist Julien Gracq to reflect on the 'icy hardness of medieval life' there. Clement, who inclined more towards the comforts of material living, had a new palace built (finished by 1348) to which he invited royalty and members of aristocratic families, entertaining them in sumptuous style. The palace was colourfully decorated. Painters from Italy as well as Provence executed much fresco work. The chapels of Saint-Martial or Saint-Jean have ceilings depicting the lives of the saints, while there are splendid scenes of hunting and other forms of recreation in the chambre du Cerf, executed with considerable skill.

The court of Clement VI must have seemed a very different place from that of Benedict. Whereas the former was cautious and economical despite his immense wealth, the latter was extravagant. Clement came to Avignon, he said, to forget that he was Pope. But he was a suspicious man and it is rumoured that he had a tunnel dug beneath the Durance from Avignon to Châteaurenard in case of emergency. And he was also responsible for initiating the construction of the walls, which are over 4 kilometres long. Clement's court attracted not only cardinals and nobility but also artists, musicians and writers from far afield. Even though Petrarch scathingly dismissed it as the 'sewer of the earth', 'the home of infidelity' and 'the habitation of demons', there can be little doubt that this was one of Avignon's most successful and colourful periods.

The town remained the property of the popes until the Revolution, when it was plundered. During the nineteenth century the papal palace was used as a prison, and then as barracks, but both it and the town in general have benefited from an extensive and quite lavish restoration programme in the years since World War 1. Apart from the palace, there is also a considerable number of other fine buildings. The twelfth-century cathedral of Notre-Dame-des-Doms (despite the unattractive addition of a gilded statue of the Virgin Mary to its tower in the last century) and the fourteenth-century church of Saint-Didier are both well worth visiting. There are also many civic and domestic buildings of much charm and interest which offer fascinating glimpses of Avignon's history. In particular, anyone visiting the town should see the fourteenth-century Petit Palais, home of the arch-bishops, the original mint, the Hôtel des Monnaies, with its ornate Italianate façade, and the medieval artisanal areas of La Balance, Les Fusteries and La Bonasterie (whose restoration has been to some extent controversial).

The bridge for which the town is universally known is outside the walls to the northwest. What remains of it is almost certainly Roman in origin, though it is likely that there was an important crossing-point of the Rhône here many years earlier. But as is so often the case, legend is more attractive. The bridge is said to have been the work of Bénézet, a young twelfth-century shepherd, after whom it is named. Some stories claim that he had already made a reputation as a builder of small bridges, but most are agreed that he was only twelve when Christ spoke to him and instructed him to undertake the work of bridging the river, and the wide area of tributaries and marshland which then fringed it. Not surprisingly, the Bishop of Avignon and the provost were sceptical, but Bénézet proved his ability (and strength) by carrying a rock, which thirty men together had failed to move, and placing it where the first arch of the bridge would be. Astonished at this feat, everyone contributed money and Bénézet was able to gather together the work-force he needed. When completed the bridge had twenty-two arches, but it was often damaged by flood-waters over the centuries and was eventually abandoned in the seventeenth century. Today only four arches remain. They are solidly designed and constructed, but so narrow as to cast doubt on whether people could have danced on top of them 'en rond', as the words of the old song claim.

Relatively quiet for most of the year, Avignon comes to life during the months of July and August when its festival of music and drama is held. Then as many as a quarter of a million people crowd into the town. This festival was started in 1947 and for many years was a modest affair, but it has now developed into one of the most lavish and expensive of the French cultural calendar, even rivalling the one held at Aix-en-Provence. The results are inevitable. It brings much needed income to the town and its surrounding region, but the true atmosphere of Avignon is temporarily destroyed. Not only busy but often extremely hot, Avignon, like Les Baux, is best avoided during the height of summer. Instead it should be visited in spring or winter when it may be battered by the wind, when the river can be relatively high and threatening, but

83

when something of its original medieval impregnability can still be sensed.

Some 25 kilometres to the south, between Avignon and Tarascon and west of La Petite Crau, is La Montagnette – the little mountain – most of which is now a protected natural area. This is an attractive, irregular ridge wooded with green oak, olive, pine and cypress trees and crossed by a number of narrow valleys, in one of which is the abbey of Saint-Michel-de-Frigolet. Before climbing up into La Montagnette, however, visit the prosperous little towns of Barbentane on its northern edge and Boulbon to the west. From the top of the Tour Angelic in Barbentane, all that remains of the castle built by the brother of Pope Urban V in the fourteenth century, there is one of the most impressive views of the Mont Ventoux away to the northeast, especially on a sharp, clear day in February when the mountain is capped with snow. The town also boasts some fine Renaissance architecture, in particular the Maison des Chevaliers with its arcades and columns. But the most striking building is the château, on the very edge of the town, which has been the property of the Puget family since the mid seventeenth century. Built of honey-coloured stone quarried across the Rhône in the department of Gard and fronted by a small formal garden, this is a fine example of the classical Provençal château. Richly decorated, it is particularly notable for its stone ceilings and plaster-work, and for the marble that was brought back from Italy by Jean-Pierre Balthazar de Puget, who was Louis XV's ambassador in Florence in the eighteenth century.

Boulbon is more modest, though a magnificent painting of *Christ*, now in the Louvre, originated here. Like Avignon, Barbentane and Tarascon, Boulbon was once a fortified frontier town, and the substantial remains of the château built around 1400 by the counts of Provence are impressive. These distant times are also recalled by the annual celebration of the new

Barbentane. The gallery at the Château de Puget-Barbentane is matched only by the one at the Château de Lourmarin.

wine, the 'procession des fioles', which takes place in the church of Saint-Marcellin in June. In this ceremony, from which women are excluded, the priest tastes and blesses the wine made the previous autumn, whereupon those present drink from their bottles. Any wine left over from the ceremony is then preserved as it is believed to have medicinal properties, particularly for those suffering from fever.

It is best to go on foot from Boulbon to the abbey of Saint-Michel, especially as this route quickly explains the source of the abbey's name. It comes from *férigoulo*, the Provençal word for thyme, which grows here in profusion. On dry days, particularly in summer, the air is heavy with its scent and, unless it has been replaced with a chemical substitute, thyme still provides the base for the Provençal liqueur Frigolet, referred to by

The four remaining arches of the bridge at Avignon and the walls of the papal palace.

Daudet in his *Lettres de mon moulin* as 'the elixir of Father Gaucher'. Like those for Chartreuse, La Vieille Cure and many other herb-based liqueurs, the recipe for Frigolet is reputedly secret and known only to a few, though the results are widely available throughout Provence.

The abbey itself, beautifully situated, was established by Benedictine monks from Montmajour to the south in the tenth century and has had a chequered history ever since. At the time of the Revolution it became the property of the State, and was subsequently used at one time as a school and at another as the centre for the preservation of Provençal literature and culture. In 1858 the buildings were bought by the Augustinian order of the Premonstrants, who made a number of additions in a heavy, neo-gothic style (the most prominent of which is the gatehouse, which jars unpleasantly with the natural surroundings). Fortunately the chapel of Notre-Dame-du-Bon-Remède survived. This building has an amazingly rich, baroque interior, including twelve paintings attributed to the school of Nicolas Mignard depicting scenes from the life of Mary. This chapel provides an interesting contrast to the more severe character of the earlier buildings, such as the restored church dedicated to St Michel, which alone makes the trip to the abbey worthwhile. For those going on to Tarascon, it is best to follow the valley southeast by road or path until it rejoins the main road from Avignon.

If the origins of Avignon are uncertain, those of Tarascon are even more so. Both the ancient Greeks and the Egyptians refer to a community on whose name the present one could be based (Ptolemy refers to Tarouskôn). But some claim that the first settlement was known as Jarnègues (the *quartier* Jarnègues still exists), others that it was called Nerluc, the dark wood. An alternative explanation is that Tarascon may well derive from the Indo-European word *tar* meaning rock (like *tor* in English), while there is also a theory that it is linked to the Provençal cult of the bull (*tauro*).

Whatever the origin of its name, Tarascon is closely linked in folk history to the legendary dragon, the *tarasque*. This terrifying beast is said to have come originally from Asia Minor and to have had its lair beneath the rock on which the castle was later built. For years it terrorized local people, attacking them on land or water without provocation and instantly devouring them. (One of the popular representations of the beast shows it with a pair of human legs dangling from its mouth, another with a human head between its jaws.) When Martha arrived proclaiming Christianity (see p. 101), the people challenged her to prove the strength of her faith by ridding them of the creature. This she did, calming it by splashing it with Holy Water and brandishing the Cross at it. Some stories relate that the locals immediately set upon the beast and chopped it into small pieces; others that Martha led it by a silken thread to the river where it threw itself in and was drowned. Whatever its end, the name of the town as we know it came into existence and the inhabitants accepted the Christian faith.

Life in Tarascon today is much less dramatic. The dragon's effigy is paraded in an annual ceremony which is usually held at the end of June. The celebrations include colourful and sometimes boisterous displays of various activities and skills by local craftsmen and members of the *confréries* (guilds). This festival, now held mainly, and sadly, for the benefit of tourists, was first institutionalized by King René in the late fifteenth century. He wanted to establish something in Tarascon that would challenge the supremacy of the famous fair of Beaucaire, held just across the river in Languedoc. This friendly rivalry created a bond as much as a rift between the towns and today they are very closely associated, proudly fronting each other across the Rhône.

Much of Beaucaire's castle has been lost, but Tarascon's has been carefully restored and is considered by many to be the finest of its kind in Provence, if not in the whole of France. Its position and appearance are dramatic. Its walls rise sheer from the river bank, and its rectangular towers still face

Abandoned habits? The monastery church at Saint-Michel-de-Frigolet.

The château of Tarascon plunging defiantly into the Rhône.

so has one of the four fortified gateways. But even so it undoubtedly has a charm of its own, partly deriving from its role as a market town serving much of the area around La Montagnette. While commercially and administratively in the shadow of Avignon and Arles, it is a useful point from which to explore west across the Rhône towards Nîmes and the Pont du Gard, or south towards Arles and the Camargue. The southern route in particular is a remarkably rich and rewarding journey. Within 5 kilometres of Tarascon there is an exquisite, small-scale example of romanesque building in the chapel of Saint-Gabriel, and only just south of that you come to Fontvieille, the village much loved by Daudet.

Once famed for its local stone, Fontvieille is best known today for its Moulin de Daudet, which stands on a small pine-clad hill to the south and is a museum to the writer's memory. Although the mill never belonged to Daudet, and the famous *Lettres de mon moulin* were largely written in Paris, his affection for Fontvieille was genuine and he often spent long periods here at the mas de Montauban. The area around Fontvieille is also full of reminders of the much more distant past, with its mix of reality and legend. There are the remnants of a Roman aqueduct, much of it shamefully neglected and almost completely stifled by thick clumps of brambles, and a number of prehistoric tombs. These can be seen on the small hill known as the Castellet and also in the areas of Bounias and Contignargues. Some especially good examples are on the Montagne de Cordes just northeast of Arles. This outcrop of rock, no more than 500 metres wide, is accessible only by a winding path. It was once an island in the swamps between Arles and Mouriès (less than 20 kilometres to the east) and was for long considered to have magic associations, a superstition which still lingers on among the locals. In addition to the prehistoric burial chamber here there is also a man-made cave known as the Grotte des Fées. This is supposed to link either with the caves beneath the abbey at Montmajour just north of Arles or with Tavèn's lair in the Val d'Enfer near Les Baux.

Montmajour, like Cordes, was once an island. The

aggressively across the water to the once threatening kingdom of France. In contrast, the round towers at the rear which overlook Provence are altogether softer and more conciliatory. The interior is similarly impressive. Superb vaulting and decorative work bear ample witness to the fact that, as the records suggest, the château lacked for nothing over the years.

In other respects Tarascon has lost some of its medieval style – the walls have long disappeared and

Daudet's mill overlooking Fontvieille: now a museum.

site is honeycombed with caves and underground passages, which were used by prehistoric man and also as a place of burial. There were Christian associations here long before the building of the present abbey. Saint Trophime is believed to have fled to Montmajour from Arles during the Roman persecutions and, quite inaccurately, it is said to be the site of the battle where Charlemagne defeated the Saracens. The massive blue-grey buildings which now stand grimly surveying the

plain away to the south date from the tenth century, when money to buy the land was given to the Benedictines by a wealthy lady from Arles. For two hundred years the monks strove to cultivate the swamps around them, eventually with success. The

89

abbey grew so rapidly in importance that the first counts of Provence chose to be buried there. But financial difficulties, general neglect, damage caused during the religious wars by groups of marauding mercenaries, and finally purchase by the State at the time of the Revolution almost spelt the end of the abbey. In the early nineteenth century Montmajour was even sold for building materials!

Fortunately such desecration did not last for long, though many of the buildings still bear the scars, and restoration work undertaken during the last hundred years is slow and has been only partly successful. Even so the abbey is well worth seeing. Although perhaps slightly less elegant than those at the abbeys of Thoronet, Sénanque and Silvacane, the chapel, cloisters and domestic quarters at Montmajour display characteristic Cistercian grandeur and austerity much in keeping with the bleakness of the site as a whole. Outside, near the unfinished dependent chapel of Sainte-Croix, tombs were cut in the solid rock for the first monks. Especially at dusk, these seem to have been only temporarily abandoned. The abbey's fourteenth-century tower dominates everything, not just a witness to centuries of violence and hardship but a reminder that Christianity was not the religion of the meek and humble alone. Only 5 kilometres away to the southwest the magnificently preserved Roman amphitheatre at Arles is a reminder of a different sort of violence. Hundreds of Christian martyrs and criminals met their deaths here. (More prosaically, a self-contained village community with as many as 200 dwellings was built inside the amphitheatre in the eighteenth century.)

While Aix, Avignon and Marseille between them dominate most aspects of Provençal life, Arles is in many ways the region's true capital. A site of prime strategic and commercial significance, it has been exploited and occupied over the centuries by neolithic tribes, Phoenicians, Greeks and Romans. It was held by the Saracens for a brief period in the eighth century. Their defeat at the hands of Charles Martel occasioned a number of epic poems – especially Ariosto's *Orlando furioso*, which inaccurately features Charlemagne as the hero of the hour. The town enjoyed considerable prosperity during the Middle Ages and since then has captivated visitors with its colourful atmosphere, its lively festivals and its young women, reputedly amongst the most beautiful in the world.

Distinguishing between legend and fact in the history of Arles is almost impossible. What is most striking about the town, even to the modern visitor, is that both pagan and Christian roots go very deep here. On the one hand there are Roman remains such as the arena, the theatre and the statue of Venus (which was discovered in the seventeenth century and is now in the Louvre). On the other there is the splendid church named after St Trophime, said to have been a disciple of St Peter and St Paul. This was built on the site of an earlier Carolingian church, and the carvings on the main door or in the cloisters (including, incidentally, one of the *tarasque*) are in themselves a magnificent illustration of the marriage of pagan and Christian cultures.

The Romans first came to Arles around 125 BC and within 500 years the town had achieved the status of second city of the Empire, becoming known as the 'Rome of the Gauls'. Its population may have been as large as 70,000 – considerably more than in the mid twentieth century. An important factor in its growth was the construction of the canal to Fos, initiated by the Consul Marius in 104 BC, which has remained in operation ever since. The town also benefited considerably as a result of Julius Caesar's gratitude half a century later. His position as emperor was threatened by Pompey whose support in Provence was centred on Marseille. As part of his campaign to quell opposition to his regime, Caesar ordered some boats from the Arles' builders who were long-renowned for their skills. The vessels were delivered in less than a month and Caesar used them successfully against Pompey. Imperial generosity was magnificent, as those monuments still in existence testify.

The roofs of Arles: the tower of the former cathedral of Saint-Trophime with the Rhône beyond.

Left **Sad departure? Fountain in the place de la République, Arles.**

Above **The arena at Arles, once the site of Roman butchery.**

Yet within 200 years the Roman presence was being threatened in a more fundamental way by Christianity. When Constantine gave recognition to the new faith early in the fourth century, it is claimed that 600 bishops came out of hiding in Arles alone! Thereafter Christianity remained firmly established despite threats and raids from marauding tribes from the east and from the Saracens. Many of the original chapels and churches are no longer standing, but the curious burial ground of Les Alyscamps (or Elysian Fields) to the southeast of the town centre can still be seen, albeit reduced in size. With its open stone coffins and church of Saint-Honorat, this is a haunting, mysterious place best seen at sunset, even though it – and its spirits – are disturbed by the proximity of the railway and by constantly passing cars. Trophime himself and many subsequent archbishops of Arles are supposed to have been buried here, and it was also a pre-Christian burial site.

But Arles is not simply a large-scale monument to a distant past, however splendid. Its historic remains are certainly prominent, but they have been accommodated with an ease and charm not found in many other historic towns in the modern world. The town's distinctive quality can be clearly sensed during the July festival. This spectacular event is notable above all for the enactment of local traditions and for displays of traditional costume, characterized by black velvet, white lace and wide-brimmed hats (and immortalized by Van Gogh). But it is not simply on festive occasions that the true spirit of Arles emerges. A market day in mid January has a special, distinctive quality about it – just as it does, for example, in Aix – while a visit, however brief, to any of the town's excellent museums instantly has the same evocative effect. Nobody who can sense that quality should be surprised that Mistral should have decided to give his Nobel Prize money to further the collection of Provençal arts and crafts in the Museon Arlaten.

Other attractions in Arles include the important festival of photography held every summer and the bull-shows staged in the arena (which can seat nearly 12,000). Somehow, and to its credit, Arles has managed to avoid becoming the kind of international but, in consequence, largely anonymous place that Avignon and Aix now are for part of the year. Tourism certainly thrives and is important economically, but the gaudy *corrida* posters on the hoardings do not reflect the true Arles, even if they contain an element of truth about the region in the town's immediate vicinity.

Beyond Arles is the Camargue with its bulls, wild horses, bird life and gypsies, a massive area of water and marshland (approximately 73,000 hectares) which is now largely protected. Thought at one time to have been an entrance to the underworld, this triangular island is fringed by the Petit Rhône, which flows into the sea just west of Saintes-Maries-de-la-Mer, and by the Grand Rhône flowing southeast from Arles. Built up over centuries with silt from these rivers, the low-lying Camargue is particularly vulnerable to the sea. Although now protected by a long barrier (*digue*), this proved to be totally ineffective against the freak storms in the summer of 1985, when two huge waves devastated camps and caravan sites up to 800 metres inland in the space of a few minutes. To the east lies the industrial complex around Fos; to the west is a long coastal area increasingly given over to the holiday industry. Some of the Camargue, especially the southeast corner, is largely devoted to the manufacture of salt, a tradition which dates back over 2000 years.

The true Camargue, however, lies in the centre. Here the upper, drier half is cultivated, with rice now an important crop, or grazed by sheep. The lower half is almost completely occupied by various *étangs*, nowhere more than 2 metres deep, of which the Etang de Vaccarès is the largest. Small settlements like L'Albaron are still on the Rhône, but others such as Saliers are now isolated, showing how the river has shifted its course over the centuries. So too do the two hundred or so *mas*. Of the two major châteaux, d'Avignon to the west and de l'Armellière overlooking the Grand Rhône to the east, the latter is by far the more spectacular. It dates from the early years of the

The sunset beauty of the Camargue.

seventeenth century and was built by Pierre de Sabatier, an officer of King Henri IV. Significantly both châteaux are on the edge of the Camargue, turning their backs on a wild unknown interior.

Access to the interior today is relatively easy. Secondary roads are mostly well made and there are many possibilities for excursions on foot, by boat, by Land Rover or, most attractively of all, on horseback. Tourism has also encouraged the maintenance of museums and information centres at places such as Pont de Rousty, Ginès, Méjanes or La Capellière. At the same time, because of its protected status, access to parts of the Camargue is either strictly controlled or forbidden altogether. Every attempt is being made to conserve the ecology of this unique region and its animal, bird and plant life. Even without any serious man-made threats, this would be a delicate and difficult task, but it is made much harder by the noise and pollution from the jets flying in and out of Marignane to the west of Marseille and by the debris from tens of thousands of unauthorized campers (*camping sauvage*).

Fortunately wild animal and reptile life is still plentiful, with large populations of boars, foxes, weasels, beavers, badgers, tree-frogs, eels, water-snakes and terrapins. The Camargue is also an important staging-post on natural migration routes for birds, which flock here in huge numbers. The pink (protected) flamingoes are the best known, but over four hundred other species have also been recorded. Centuries old juniper trees, remnants of the thick woods which covered the area in the Middle Ages, can still be found in the Bois de Rièges area, and carpets of amazingly colourful wild flowers can make the Camargue seem quite exceptionally beautiful at times. But there is also a hostile and inhospitable Camargue, desperately hot and humid in summer and battered by winds in autumn and winter, a place which seems scarcely to have changed from the one described in a survey commissioned by the Archbishop of Arles in 1635:

Horses of the Camargue.

Throughout the island the only water that is drunk comes from the Rhône and when the river is low farmers have to walk as far as two leagues for it. The winds are unbearable. The heat is overwhelming for four or five months in the summer. During three or four weeks there are also flies, millions of them – called *arabi* in Provençal – which drive you to distraction. They sting terribly. In most farmsteads there is no courtyard, the house is open to all weathers. There are people who have never set eyes on a priest in ten or a dozen years and have never been to mass or confession.

Obviously some things have improved – there is now irrigation, piped water and insect control (though mosquitoes are still a nuisance). But with the exception of those who live in Saintes-Maries or who work in the salt industry, the rest of the population (about 5000) seem to have a way of life that has not changed much over the centuries. Their *mas*, apart from those prepared for tourists, are still basic, almost primitive; so too are the single-storey *cabanes*, the thatched cob dwellings of the bull herdsmen (the *gardians*), often built defiantly to face the mistral and crowned by a bull's horn to ward off evil spirits.

The black, sprightly Camargue bulls, like the white horses, are held in high esteem. Their origins are unknown. Some claim that both animals derive from Central Asia; others that the horses are a special strain directly descended from the same prehistoric ancestor as the common European horse; others again point out the resemblance between the Camargue bulls and those painted in the Lascaux caves. Though now fewer in number than three hundred years ago, both animals have retained a mystical quality: the horses because of their independent spirit, unique colouring (black at birth, they take three years to turn fully white), strength and fine stature; the bulls because of their mythological links with Mithra, the Iranian God of Light, who was adopted by the Romans as protector of their Empire. Both are associated with a series of rituals and a language for the initiated only. In a way they epitomize the whole region and few sights are more impressive or evocative than a herd (*manade*) of bulls or horses, cutting through the swamps as though impelled by an independent and unseen spirit. Roy

Left Fos. Not far from here are medieval tombs carved out of rock.

Above The fortified church of Notre-Dame at Saintes-Maries-de-la-Mer, which houses the relics of Mary Jacoby, Mary Salome and Sara.

Campbell once called them the 'sons of the mistral'.

Whatever pagan forces motivate these aspects of the Camargue, Saintes-Maries-de-la-Mer is the source of many of the Christian practices, legends and beliefs which permeate Provence as a whole. There was a settlement at or near the present site of the town well over two thousand years ago, even before the arrival of the Greeks, and some believe Saintes-Maries may have Egyptian associations. But the modern town owes its name to the arrival of a boat in AD 40, with neither oars nor sail, bearing a group of Christians who had been persecuted and set adrift from Palestine by the Jews. These Christians included Mary Jacoby (sister of the Virgin Mary); Mary Salome (mother of the saints John and James); Sara their servant; Lazarus and his sisters Mary Magdalene and Martha; Maximinus and Sidonius.

The first three remained to establish a Christian community; the others dispersed into Provence and Martha subsequently arrived in Tarascon where she had her encounter with the dragon (see p. 87). Nowadays their arrival is re-enacted in two major and colourful *fêtes*: the first takes place on 24 and 25 May and attracts gypsies from all over Europe. (Sara is their patron saint, though an all-night candle-lit vigil held in her honour in the church has been banned since 1955.) The second, devoted to Mary Salome, is on the Sunday nearest to 22 October. The relics of Mary Jacoby, Mary Salome and Sara (discovered, it is claimed, in 1448) and their effigies hang in a chapel in the apse of the fortified church of Notre-Dame-de-la-Mer. This imposing, rather sombre building has suffered at the hand of man, especially at the time of the Revolution, as much as from the harshness of the climate here. To visit it at the height of the tourist season can be uncomfortable, but to do so at night in midwinter when the moonlight is reflected and diffused by both sea and inland water is an altogether different experience. Then the whole village appears luminous and almost supernatural, an island surrounded by silence and mystery.

The journey back to Marseille 120 kilometres to the east requires a long detour northwards through the salt production areas and thence across the industrial wasteland bordering the Golfe de Fos. Fos itself – a *village perché* reached by a magnificent drive through pine trees – has managed to retain its character (just), despite the extensive industrial development around it. Similarly, only 10 kilometres away, the three linked parishes of Martigues (*eaux mortes*: dead waters) at the mouth of the Etang de Berre still have enormous charm. Many artists were attracted here in the nineteenth century, including Corot and the Burgundian Félix Ziem, whose evocative painting of the Vieux Port in Marseille hangs in the town's art gallery.

From Martigues back to Marseille by motorway along the southern edge of the Etang is only a matter of minutes. A more leisurely and attractive route, however, is to make for L'Estaque and follow the coast, preferably by local train. The line weaves round rocky inlets and passes through pretty, fashionable villages such as Sausset-les-Pins, Carry-le-Rouet or Niolon. L'Estaque itself was much visited by Cézanne, and later became a haven for the Cubists. It is now merely an extension of Marseille and little more than a harbour for boats of all sizes and descriptions. In fact, Marseille re-asserts itself quickly. Nevertheless, despite all the bustle, noise, brashness and dirt of its modern industry and commerce, it cannot destroy that special atmosphere created by a blend of history, tradition and magic which so strongly infuses its immediate hinterland.

Fishing port at Martigues.

Avignon

Sénas Mallemort Cadenet
Alleins Silvacane
Vernègues La Roque-
d'Anthéron
Lambesc Durance
Pélissanne Rognes Meyrargues
Venelles Rians St-Martin Varages Aups
Vauvenargues Le Puits- Esparron
de-Rians Barjols
Aix-en- Le Tholonet Montagne Sainte
Arc Provence Victoire
Puyloubier Pourrières Argens
Bouc-Bel-Air Fuveau Seillons-Source-d'Argens
Cabriès Gardanne Trets St-Maximin-la-Ste-Baume
St-Zacharie Rougiers Tourves Brignoles
Auriol Massif de la Baume Mazaugues
Sainte Baume La Roquebrussane
Plan-d'Aups Nans-les-Pins
L'Estaque Gémenos Méounes-
Marseille les-Montrieux Massif des
Aubagne Gapeau Maures
Cuges-les-Pins
Cassis Le Castellet St-Tropez
Les Le Revest-les-Eaux
Lecques St-Cyr-sur-Mer
La Ciotat Bandol Toulon Hyères
Ile de Bendor Sanary-
sur-Mer
Six-Fours-les-Plages
Le Brusc St-Mandrier-
sur-Mer
Les Sablettes Ile de Port-Cros

Mediterranean

3
Aix and its Environs

Aix – Montagne Sainte Victoire – Mallemort –
Aubagne – Massif de la Sainte Baume – Trets –
Saint-Maximin – Rians – Brignoles – Cassis –
La Ciotat – Bandol

If Marseille is the commercial and business centre of Provence, Aix, no more than 30 kilometres away, has long claimed to be the artistic and cultural one. With the growth of music and theatre festivals elsewhere, especially during the summer months, this claim is perhaps less strong than it once was. But Aix undeniably still has charm and character, which are jealously preserved and cultivated, even if a degree of pretentiousness has crept in in recent years. There is no doubt either that the town is given a certain intellectual prestige by its flourishing university. First established in the early fifteenth century, this is now one of the most important in France. Even though today's population of over 120,000 is the result of a fourfold increase since the late 1950s (with nearly 10,000 people arriving from North Africa alone after the Algerian War), there is still a feeling among those who live in Aix, including many who consider themselves to be genuine *aixois*, that they belong to an élite even by national standards. The poet Blaise Cendrars, who went to live there in 1940 following the German invasion of the north of France, summed things up well. In Aix, he said, he found 'small shop keepers, dreadful middle-class people, heavily made-up women, bluestockings and intellectuals who frequented the *Deux Garçons* café on the Cours Mirabeau'. Yet justified though his reaction may have been, it is easy to be dismissive (and jealous) of a town which has so many natural advantages, even if it is in danger of spoiling some of them by seemingly thoughtless residential development.

From Marseille the main routes north to Aix pass between the Chaîne de Vitrolles and the more extensive and larger Chaîne de l'Etoile. Though largely denuded by forest fires, the stony chalk slopes of L'Etoile offer some stiff walking and climb to over 600 metres. The views from the col Sainte Anne and the Grande Etoile, either west towards the Etang de Berre or south over the urban sprawl of Marseille, are spectacular. And the tiny community of Cabriès, with its castle and church, is typical of many *villages perchés* in this area, including Bouc-Bel-Air which it faces across the valley on the eastern side of the A51. Otherwise there is little of immediate interest on this route; pockets of industrial development, quarries and mines scar the landscape and pollute the atmosphere. Going into Aix too from this direction is to see the town's least attractive side, with a battery of apartment blocks. Some are pleasantly designed, attractively painted and very expensive; others all too recognizably bear the marks of budget building and show signs of wear.

Curiously enough one of the best vantage points from which to observe these attempts to cope with a

growing population is the Fondation Vasarely, conceived by the Hungarian himself in 1976 as a centre for research into the ways in which artificial, plastic beauty will, inevitably, replace that of nature. The Fondation building is large and imaginative. Made of aluminium, it is designed in six hexagonal blocks, though its size is cleverly 'reduced' by the external decor – a series of severe façades on which circles on squares in black alternate with the same thing in white, like the positive and negative qualities of a film. The Fondation houses a permanent exhibition of Vasarely's work, a bewildering display of strange dimensions and shifting perspectives, and there is also an illustrated *résumé* of his theories and ideas. A little ironically the Fondation lies in a suburb known as Jas-de-Bouffon, so-called after the large house in which Cézanne, the most famous of Provençal painters, spent much of his early life.

The heart of Aix lies to the northeast of the hill on which the Fondation stands. The city is built in a natural basin, indisputably one of the best sites in France. Sheltered from the wind except when the mistral blows at its fiercest, with abundant water from local springs and shaded by immense and ubiquitous plane trees, it enjoys a Mediterranean micro-climate of the most agreeable kind. To sit outside one of the cafés in the Cours Mirabeau on a warm spring morning, or to stroll through the Parc Jourdain towards the modern university buildings on a hot summer day listening to the sound of fountains and garden-sprays, can be unforgettable experiences, however prosaic. And the town is still visited for its warm, mineral-rich springs which have made it an internationally famous spa.

The history of Aix dates back well over two thousand years. Just to the north, on the plateau of Entremont, are the remains of an extensive fortified town established by the Salyens, which was then sacked by the Romans in 123 BC. (Many of the relics excavated here, including a number of curious stone

---

There is no need for this water to carry a health warning.

effigies of death-heads, can be seen in the Granet Museum.) The Roman consul Sextius then set up his own community around the springs (which the Salyens believed could improve the fertility of their women). From that moment the town's present name evolved: *Aquae Sextius*, the waters of Sextius.

Unlike many other towns in Provence, Aix has little evidence of early Roman settlement today, though the remains of one of the principal gateways can be seen at the base of the sixteenth-century tower with the ornate astrological clock in the place de l'Hôtel de Ville. There is rather more to be seen of the medieval city, especially around the cathedral of Saint-Sauveur, whose severely austere baptistry dates from the fourth century and whose twelfth-century cloisters bear comparison with those of Saint-Trophime in Arles. Here, in an area partly rebuilt in the seventeenth century, are narrow streets, tiny, hidden courtyards and heavily shuttered houses – all in the best Provençal style.

In the Middle Ages the town became the principal residence for the counts of Provence, of whom René (1434–80) was perhaps the most famous. He it was who encouraged the development of the arts here and made Aix into a cultural centre worthy to be compared with Avignon. During the next 250 years the town's fortunes varied. It suffered from wars, religious disputes and disease, while local opposition to the centralizing government of Louis XIV prompted a visit by the Sun King himself in 1660.

Although still wracked internally by political and religious rivalries and debates, Aix began to develop into the town we know today from the seventeenth century. Social pretensions, inspired here, as else-where in France, by Louis' court at Versailles, led to the construction of a number of sumptuous private residences and public buildings (some of which were not completed for nearly 200 years). The old town hall (now housing the superb Méjanes library), the law faculty opposite the cathedral, the place d'Albertas, the Pavillon de Vendôme, and the 143 listed magnificent town houses (*hôtels*), with their elaborate carvings and wrought ironwork, are all products of

Left Classical elegance and torment. Puget's caryatids on the Pavillon de Vendôme in Aix.

Above Not another photographer. . . . Detail from the Pavillon de Vendôme.

107

this new period of prosperity. The mid seventeenth century also saw the demolition of the town's southern fortifications and the creation of the Cours Mirabeau in their place in 1651. As one contemporary put it, this was intended to be a 'social theatre where people of good breeding' could meet and mix in comfort – though the appearance of the first cafés caused a public outcry!

Those who consider themselves fashionable still spend entire afternoons and evenings walking up and down the Cours (*faire le Cours*), or sitting in one of the cafés, all of which are carefully placed in the social hierarchy. Cendrars' reaction is understandable, but especially during the summer there is something uniquely attractive about this part of Aix. The Cours is turned into a pedestrian precinct on a number of occasions in July and early August, and is used for open-air concerts and exhibitions as well as street markets. Tourists flock to the town in their tens of thousands, just as they do to Avignon or Arles, but Aix is far better placed to cope with this influx than its neighbours. The generous scale of the streets and buildings guarantees a certain dignity, which is enhanced by the magnificent plane trees and the refreshing presence of the fountains (to which flocks of sheep were once brought for watering).

With no industrial development of any significance in the nineteenth century, Aix was spared the massive urban expansion experienced by Marseille. The atmosphere of the town remained much the same and new buildings reflected the growth of intellectual and cultural activities. Likewise the population varied little from the mid eighteenth century to the mid twentieth – remaining around 30,000. Since then, with rapid expansion, things have changed, and it is striking that over a third of the population is of or below student age. It is unlikely that Aix will ever suffer from the kinds of inner city problems which have developed in Marseille, but similar ones have begun to manifest themselves in some of the less elegant and less prestigious suburbs. Here there is vandalism and walls are sprayed with slogans, many of them strongly nationalistic and racist in tone, and

there is no doubt that the incidence of social unrest is increasing. Paradoxically, the very laudable attempt to preserve the character of the old town is to some extent responsible. Creating pedestrian areas and restoring old buildings is an expensive business and rates and rents have risen dramatically as a result, obliging many former inhabitants to move to the outer areas.

To the casual visitor, however, the centre of Aix has an elegance which rivals that to be found in parts of the Latin Quarter in Paris. And its markets are arguably the best in Provence. Not only do these offer the usual fruit, vegetables, cheeses and local bread, but also genuine bargains on the stalls selling antiques and books. As in most places in Provence, the markets are legally obliged to close at midday, when children and beggars scavenge amongst the discarded boxes for damaged produce, drawing attention to another world lurking only just below the surface.

This social gap is perhaps most apparent during the festival weeks when Aix, like Avignon, becomes a different, cosmopolitan place. Then it is even more colourful than usual, but it is also expensive and exclusive. For those who can afford the ticket prices, Mozart's *Don Giovanni* presented on a warm evening in the open courtyard of the Archbishop's Palace, or Haydn's *Creation* in the cathedral can be deeply moving experiences, but many – indeed most – have to be content with free displays of folk-dancing, juggling or over-priced local crafts. Yet few who come to Aix can resist its magic. From his statue at the eastern end of the Cours Mirabeau, King René looks benignly upon the faithful who return year after year and thus ensure the continued prosperity of his town.

In addition to its own special qualities, Aix is also ideally placed for a variety of excursions in all directions. Perhaps the most popular is the one which leads east towards Vauvenargues through the suburb of Repentance, much of which is still a thickly wooded

The château at Vauvenargues in a blaze of autumn colour. Picasso is buried here.

area topped by an old fourteenth-century look-out post, the Tour de César. Here as elsewhere residential development is gradually eating into the countryside, but the forests to the south of the road are protected by government order, ensuring, at least for the time being, that the true character of the area will be preserved. Not far out of Aix the road passes two dams, the Barrage Zola (designed and built by the novelist's father) and the Barrage de Bimont. The two lakes behind them are the principal source of water for the ever-growing town only a few kilometres away. Although these lakes are far less spectacular than those in the Gorges du Verdon to the northeast, they form a striking foreground to the Sainte Victoire range. For those who like walking, there are a number of well-marked paths of varying degrees of difficulty across the mountains. Another attractive spot is the tiny hamlet of Saint-Marc-Jaumegarde, on the same side of the road as the lakes, whose sixteenth-century château can just be glimpsed through the tops of the pine and cypress trees.

Less than 5 kilometres further on the road enters the much restored village of Vauvenargues. The château here was built between the fourteenth and seventeenth centuries and was originally owned by the Vauvenargues family, whose most distinguished member, Luc (1715–47), became known as a philosophical writer and was befriended by Voltaire. But the many tourists who come to photograph the château are interested in a more recent inhabitant. In 1958 it was bought by Picasso who, even though he was to spend relatively little time there, chose it as his burial place. The château contains a number of his works, notably his variations on Manet's famous *Déjeuner sur l'herbe*, but unfortunately it is not open to the public. Nevertheless, it is well worth simply viewing it from the road as it sits sturdily amongst the oaks and box trees at the foot of the northern slopes of Sainte Victoire.

Just beyond the château is one of the easier paths leading to the top of the Sainte Victoire and the Croix de Provence. The magnificent limestone range, 7 kilometres long, dominates the entire area. The name

Sainte Victoire, which commemorates the victory of Marius over the invading Germanic tribes in 102 BC, dates from the seventeenth century. Previously it had been known as the Mont Ventour or windy mountain, like the much higher Mont Ventoux to the north. The relatively gentle slopes on the northern side can be climbed comfortably within two hours, and on a fine day the views from the summit (nearly 1000 metres) are superb, both north towards the Lubéron or south over the valley of the river Arc to the Massif de la Sainte Baume. A pilgrimage is made every April to the remains of a priory on the mountain, and this and a stone-built shelter – often a site for *camping sauvage* – provide walkers with some protection from the wind, which can blow here in formidable gusts. On the southern side of the mountain there is an almost sheer drop of some 500 metres which must be approached with caution. Starkly white on some days, grey, violet or golden on others, sometimes etched two-dimensionally against a brilliant blue sky, at others shrouded in mist, the mountain appears to respond to the weather in an amazingly sensitive manner – little wonder that Cézanne should have become increasingly obsessed by it.

Those who are hardy can walk the length of the crest and cross the range to descend into the village of Puyloubier. But the road from Vauvenargues which runs parallel to the mountain ridge and plunges through the valley of the Infernet is equally rewarding, especially if it is followed south from Le-Puits-de-Rians to Pourrières. Here the scenery changes abruptly. The harsh terrain, ochre-coloured soil and forest of the eastern end of the mountain range give way to the fertile plain which is crossed by the Arc and its tributaries. Market gardening and vines are much in evidence. Pourrières is today largely occupied by *vignerons*, but one tradition has it that its name derives from *campi porrerias* – fields of leeks. Another, less attractive story suggests it was the site of Marius' famous victory, and that the dead bodies of the Germanic tribes were left to rot on the ground, hence *campi putridi*. . . .

From Pourrières the road climbs back towards the

Sainte Victoire. Did Cézanne paint this view?

became so fascinated by it. For him the mountain came to epitomize all that was unique in the countryside and atmosphere of Provence, of which he set himself to be the interpreter (*'le paysage se pense en moi'*). Noted for his shyness and for his dislike of being watched as he painted, Cézanne had studios in several different and normally secluded parts of Provence, or in family properties – the Jas de Bouffan, L'Estaque, Gardanne, Châteaunoir and Le Tholonet. Cézanne painted his mountain more than a hundred times during the last ten years of his life, and on the road back into Aix it is easy to imagine the views that inspired him.

The second excursion from Aix is on a smaller scale and quite different in character. Going north in the direction of Meyrargues, this route passes through the area of Les Pinchinats, a name derived from *penchinat*, the Provençal for carding and a reminder of the linen industry for which Aix was once famous. Almost at once the road reaches the first of three notable châteaux in this well-watered area – the Pavillon de l'Enfant, surrounded by its lawns and fountains and shaded by massive chestnut and lime trees. The château, the smallest and externally the least inspiring of the three, was named after Simon Lenfant, general treasurer of France in 1674, and was clearly built in two stages. The ground and first floors date from the seventeenth century (1683); the second was added in the eighteenth and is marked off by a stone frieze. The optical effect is to make the house seem higher than it actually is.

The interior is unusually rich for a house of this kind, with ornate plaster-work chimney-pieces and door canopies. The wrought ironwork in the stairwell is especially fine and a statue of Fame heralding visitors on a trumpet stands at the head of the staircase. There are also two baroque frescoes dating from the eighteenth century attributed to Jean-Baptiste Van Loo, who purchased the Pavillon de Vendôme in Aix around 1730. Of these, the one depicting Apollo and the gods in the *grand salon* on the first floor was supposedly completed in less than three weeks. The château was leased to the Church by Lenfant's last descendant at the end of the eighteenth century, but

southern face of Sainte Victoire by way of Puyloubier, Saint-Antonin and Le Bouquet, eventually reaching Le Tholonet only 5 kilometres from Aix. Le Tholonet is not a particularly interesting village, but is worth visiting for its seventeenth-century Italianate château. Since 1959, somewhat incongruously, this has been the administrative centre for the Société du Canal de Provence, but this has not detracted from its splendour and the château is in an excellent state of preservation. The original main carriage-way – now a car-park on the other side of the road – can still be seen leading up between twin rows of plane trees. The château looks at its best during the Aix festival when the grounds, floodlit for the occasion, provide an elegant setting for open-air concerts.

The road from Pourrières to Le Tholonet is dominated all the way by the presence of Sainte Victoire and it is worth following this route in order to understand why Cézanne (who died in Aix in 1906)

was finally purchased by a private buyer in 1955 and is immaculately maintained.

Further north the road soon penetrates one of the most beautiful rural suburbs of Aix. Much of the area is under cultivation (growing the ubiquitous olive, grapes, and some grain), but the long, shaded drives which disappear into the pines and oaks from sturdy, firmly-locked gates indicate some of the most elegant and expensive modern houses of the region. Here also are the two other châteaux which are worth visiting – La Mignarde and La Gaude – both privately owned like the Pavillon.

La Mignarde is the less elegant of the two, the large front terrace appearing almost cluttered by statues of animals and classical human figures. Dating from the late eighteenth century (1775), it was originally simply a *bastide* and was extended by Jean-Sauveur Mignard, the son of a confectioner employed by the last governor of Provence, the Maréchal de Villars. Unfortunately his ambitions outstripped his financial resources and he became bankrupt, the house subsequently passing through various hands. In 1807 Napoleon's strong-minded sister Pauline stayed here and is said to have bathed in milk – her marble bath is still to be seen. Such an exotic pastime was in keeping with much of the interior decoration for which Mignard was responsible, including the wall hangings (those in the dining-room depict the cultivation of rice in China), the ornate plaster-work and a domed boudoir. There is also a splendid example of a *radassière*, a form of divan introduced into Provence from the Middle East and used as a shaded conversation area during the heat of the day. Externally, though, despite the ornamental lake and the dual rows of fine plane trees, exoticism gives way to an atmosphere of genteel decay.

Quite the reverse is true of the château of La Gaude, whose grounds adjoin those of La Mignarde. Approached by a narrow, tunnel-like driveway, this delightful Italianate château was built early in the eighteenth century for Charles Pisani de la Gaude who planned to offer it to his intended wife as a token of his love. Unfortunately, but in the best romantic tradition, she died on the eve of their wedding and la Gaude entered Holy Orders, eventually becoming Bishop of Vence. In the ensuing century and a half the house had mixed fortunes, changing hands with some regularity until, in 1938, it was purchased by the Baron de Vitrolles. It is presently owned by his son and daughter-in-law, and they and the baron have been largely responsible for its restoration and maintenance.

A terrace in front of the house is guarded by two sculptured dogs attributed to the Aix artist Jean Chastel and overlooks a symmetrical maze of dwarf box hedges surrounded by water. From here paths lead down to a series of stepped lawns and pools flanked by cypress and yew trees. The view of the house from the very bottom of these formal gardens is impressive, its mellow, honey-coloured stone and fine windows being seen to their best advantage in the full sunlight of summer or when floodlit. There are shaded walks and resting places on either side, and the grounds also contain a small Louis XVI chapel, an orangery, and, to the rear of the house, outhouses and stables with a traditional dovecote. Unfortunately the interior is not open to the public, but La Gaude as a whole is an exquisite example of classical Provençal taste, standing almost aloof from the wild landscape of the Chaîne de l'Etoile which it faces away to the south.

For those who want to go further afield, more extensive excursions to the north, east and southeast of Aix take in regions of very different character. Beyond the city to the northwest the N7 leads anonymously and unattractively towards Sénas and thence to Avignon, but minor roads on either side wander past a number of *bastides* and substantial houses, a reminder that the wealthy middle classes of Aix and Marseille once had their country retreats in this region. Several of them now function as wine châteaux and are linked by a clearly marked *route des vins*. Eguilles, no more than 10 kilometres from Aix and overlooking the valley of the Arc, Pélissanne and

Avenue of plane trees: Le Tholonet.

Lambesc are all interesting examples of large villages with some fine town houses, the best of them comparing favourably with those in Aix itself.

About half-way between Pélissanne and Lambesc is the fortified château of La Barben. Much and not always tastefully restored since the Middle Ages, La Barben was sold by King René to the Forbin family in the mid fifteenth century. Originally Marseille merchants, the Forbins became one of the most noble households of all Provence. The best known member of the family is Auguste, who was Pauline Bonaparte's lover during her stay at La Mignarde. When in Rome several years later, his charms so attracted Juliette Récamier that the French writer and politician Benjamin Constant was provoked into challenging him to a duel. Fortunately it failed to take place and Auguste was able to devote the rest of his life to painting. But despite such romantic associations and a superb site on an outcrop of rock amongst rich pine forests, La Barben now has to rely for its survival on the most incongruous of commercial ventures – a wildlife park and a miniature railway.

The road directly north from Pélissanne through Aurons, Vernègues and Alleins is wooded and attractive (and there are some interesting remains of a Roman temple near Vernègues). Occasionally there are glimpses of the Canal EDF (Electricité de France), which leads up to the hydro-electric stations near Mallemort on the Durance. Invaluable though this source of power is, the operation of the stations plays havoc with the river's levels and it is dangerous for swimmers and fishermen alike. For much of the time, except in winter or after very heavy rain, the Durance is little more than a series of linked grey pools and large pebble beds, but its potential force and speed are shown only too clearly by the smooth, whitened branches and trunks of riverside trees.

Mallemort itself is one of Provence's *villages perchés*, its inhabitants working either for EDF or on the rich alluvial soil of the river valley. A few kilometres to the east the small community of La Roque-d'Anthéron is more interesting. This village was laid out in its present symmetrical form by the Forbin family in the sixteenth century and two centuries later another powerful family, the Cadenet, created a form of commune incorporating seventy families.

La Roque lies on an attractive strip of land caught between the Durance at one of its narrowest points and the wooded hills of the Chaîne des Côtes to the south. Once an area of marsh, people are drawn here now principally because of the abbey at Silvacane (*silva cannorum*: wood of reeds).

This Cistercian monastery was founded in 1144 during St Bernard's lifetime. Built over a period of about four hundred years, it is a good if not outstanding example of its kind. The fundamental simplicity of the original design is still clearly apparent despite the mixture of styles, and, together with the abbey's rural setting, invites reflection and repose. Yet Silvacane was only saved from destruction by State intervention in the mid nineteenth century. After the Revolution the abbey was virtually abandoned and was sold as a farm. Like its great medieval rival to the west, the Benedictine Montmajour, Silvacane became a useful source of building materials and only enforced purchase ensured that it was not entirely demolished. Today it is a much visited historic monument and is also occasionally used for concerts. Whether by chance or design, the acoustic is of the highest quality and unaccompanied choral music here can be deeply haunting.

The quickest route back to Aix from Silvacane is along the Durance as far as Meyrargues, and thence south through Venelles and Les Pinchinats. It is worth making a short detour just a few kilometres before Meyrargues in order to see the château of Fonscolombe, isolated between a small side road and the canal. Neither house nor grounds are open, but the château can be seen clearly from the road and is an interesting, if rather severe example of eighteenth-century architecture and landscape gardening. Meyrargues and Venelles are both pleasantly sited and Meyrargues

'*Le petit tambour d'Archole*' at **Cadenet near Mallemort.**

still has some traces of its Roman past. Material from the remains of the important aqueduct here was used in the construction of the thirteenth-century château.

But a more picturesque route is to take any of the more minor roads across the Massif de la Trévaresse. These hills rise quite steeply to about 500 metres. They are well worth traversing for their range of scenery: dark-brown, almost black basalt soil in some parts, rich green river gorges thickly covered with woods on the north face, with bleaker, more windswept valleys to the west. In 1909 this area was the epicentre of an earthquake which shook much of Provence and ruined or damaged most of the local villages. The community of Rognes, clustered on the hillside beneath its ruined château, was finally abandoned at that time, but the village is still famous throughout the region for the warm, beautifully grained honey-coloured stone that was produced from its quarries. This stone lives on in many an elegant seventeenth- and eighteenth-century town house. Now disused, the quarries are also worth exploring. Like certain areas of the Sainte Baume range, the rock contains considerable numbers of fossils, though these are not of very good quality. The Massif de la Trévaresse has so far been spared the damage inflicted elsewhere by forest fires, and is a most attractive pocket of Provençal countryside. Just how long it will remain so, however, is difficult to say, as more and more village houses and parcels of land are bought up by people from Aix.

The same phenomenon is happening elsewhere around Aix: to the east around Sainte Victoire and towards Saint-Maximin and Brignoles, or down towards the coast almost as far as Toulon. These developments are partly due to the motorway system, which has brought more people out of Marseille into villages around, especially those on the northern side of the Massif de la Sainte Baume. It has also improved access to many small coastal resorts, which are now heavily congested in summer, while those who are willing to undertake the journey can now use the A8 to work in the Aix-Marseille conglomeration, while living up to 100 kilometres away in the hinterland of Le Lavandou and Saint-Tropez. This changing pattern

of communications has had two quite different consequences in the immediate vicinity of Aix. Firstly, where the old road from Aix to Nice and Toulon crosses the hills immediately south of the city, some of the land that borders it is once more being used for agriculture (goat farming and the cultivation of lavender). The second is the view of Fuveau – a perfectly shaped Provençal village – that has been opened up from the new motorway link (the A52) running down to the Pas-de-Trets.

Change for the better is slow, however, and the villages on the main road between Aix and Aubagne just east of Marseille have little that is attractive about them. Yet as people move out of Marseille a new prosperity is becoming evident. This is particularly true of Aubagne itself, once a place of summer residence for the bishops of Marseille and now a small market town in the fertile region overlooked to the east by the mountains of the Sainte Baume and to the west by the imposing hump of rock of the Garlaban. A natural centre for many local peasant farmers, the town is at its most colourful on market days. Of its other claims to fame, the most curious is perhaps the museum of the Foreign Legion, where the withered hand of the Legion's founder is displayed. Aubagne is also the birthplace of Marcel Pagnol (1895–1974), whose novels, plays and films (such as *Fanny, César* or *Topaze*) have immortalized many aspects of Provençal life, though not without some glib romanticism. Like Nostradamus at Salon, Pagnol is a local celebrity and has inspired clubs, societies and a permanent exhibition in his honour. There are also 'favourite Pagnol' walks organized through the local hills, heavy with wild thyme and rosemary, but increasingly ravaged by fires. And there are the *santons*.

These figurines are said to have been brought to France in the eighteenth century by traders from Italy. Originally religious in inspiration, they were representations of saints made from wood, cork, glass or

The pale, locally-quarried stone at Rognes.

wax and were widely used in models of the Nativity. Banned in churches after the Revolution, a Marseille craftsman, Jean-Louis Laguel, had the idea of reproducing them in quantity for people to celebrate their faith in their own homes. The local clay proved to be ideally suited to the production of these figurines and Aubagne quickly became the centre of the craft, though it is now practised throughout Provence as a whole. Over the years the range of characters has broadened to include many Provençal types that are not religious in inspiration and which often have traditional names. These highly coloured figures can be purchased from the studios of individual artists or during the permanent summer exhibition in the town square.

Once away from the main road this whole inland area to the southeast of Aix offers countless opportunities for excursions by car or on foot. It is dominated by the highest of the Provençal ranges, the Massif de la Sainte Baume, which has a commanding, central position like that of the Sainte Victoire further to the north. It is possible to circle the Massif completely, passing through a series of villages which each deserve more than a fleeting visit. From Aubagne the road goes east via Gémenos and Cuges-les-Pins to Méounes-les-Montrieux, then north to Tourves via La Roquebrussane and back west along the attractive valley of the Huveaune through Rougiers, Saint-Zacharie and Auriol. Of these villages, Gémenos has the greatest claim to fame. It is known as the *Versailles Marseillais* because Le Nôtre was partly responsible for the château and its formal gardens.

The first part of this excursion is dominated by the steep sides of the mountain, but the return journey is through a narrow, fertile and intensively cultivated plain. This circular trip is well worth doing, but the smaller roads and forest tracks which lead into the Massif itself are more rewarding. From Gémenos the

This is known locally in Aubagne as the clock tower.

road winds breathtakingly up through the Col de l'Espigoulier, where it meets another rising from Auriol to the north. Once covered by pines, the land on the southern side of the Massif now resembles a sinister charred desert – the result of one of the worst local fires of the 1970s. From the junction of the two roads at La Coutronne, there are countless possibilities for walks. In summer, some of the best lie along the waterless river beds where the sandstone has been carved into fantastic shapes by fierce winter torrents over the centuries. Insect life, especially butterflies and dragonflies, is plentiful and the north face of the range has a greater variety of trees and bushes than in any other part of Provence. Privet, beech, yew, pine, maple, oak and lime trees grow in profusion, as do ferns and wild flowers, giving the impression that you are walking through a wood in northern Europe rather than one in southern France.

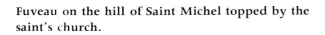

Fuveau on the hill of Saint Michel topped by the saint's church.

Climbing from Gémenos towards the Col de l'Espigoulier.

Preservation orders here are strictly enforced, ensuring that the wood is not damaged. Elsewhere parts of the forest are almost impenetrable and anyone walking in these areas should take great care, especially if there is any danger of bad weather. It can be bitterly cold in winter and people in local villages, like those in the Mont Ventoux region, still recall how the local climate was put to good use in the days before modern refrigeration. People would cut blocks of ice, drop them into wells or ice-houses insulated with hay and then transport them by horse and cart to Marseille when the spring came, a journey which could take two to three days! A number of areas known as Les Glacières are so-called for this reason and there are still ice-houses to be found.

From La Coutronne the road runs east parallel to the steepest part of the mountain and overlooked by some sinister telecommunications sites. At the eastern end of the range, the road divides, one branch leading to Nans-les-Pins, the other to Mazaugues and the area of bauxite mining. Before that, however, the delightful romanesque church at Plan-d'Aups should not be missed, and it is well worth walking up through the forest from the Hostellerie de la Sainte-Baume (now an ecumenical youth centre) to the grotto that is only 100 metres or so below the summit.

The story of this grotto is central to Provençal Christian mythology. Mary Magdalene, having arrived at Saintes-Maries-de-la-Mer, turned her evangelizing attentions towards this part of Provence, in particular the valley of the Huveaune. Legend has it that she was eventually carried by angels to the cave where she was to live for 33 years, partly as penance for her attachment to the beauty of the flesh. As death approached she was once more carried by angels, this time to Saint-Maximin, where her relics are now found (despite the fact they were claimed over the centuries by rival monks at Vézelay). The grotto was inaccessible for hundreds of years, but it has been a place of pilgrimage since the thirteenth century at least and has been in the charge of the Dominican order from the mid nineteenth century. It is associated with fertility in local folklore and is said still to be visited by young women who have difficulty in conceiving. Those who make the effort to walk up to the grotto, and the intrepid who go beyond it to Saint Pilon and the crest of the mountain, will be rewarded by the view north beyond Aix to the Lubéron and, on clear days, the Mont Ventoux.

Although less than 50 kilometres from Marseille, Aix or Toulon, it is amazing how basic living conditions still are for the many people who live isolated from any of the major villages in the Sainte-Baume region. As in any mountainous area, there are enormous problems in connecting remote settlements to mains water, drainage or electricity. And even in some villages which are now witnessing rapid and not

The desolate beauty of the countryside around Plan-d'Aups.

Provençal pumpkins near Plan-d'Aups.

always attractive secondary development, such as Auriol and Saint-Zacharie, there are still signs that not long ago they were essentially peasant communities. Rabbits and hens may still be kept in the ground-floor room of old village houses, and here too fruit and vegetables are sorted and prepared for market.

Life in the forested mountainous region to the south between the southern slopes of the Sainte Baume and Toulon is very similar. But main roads provide easy access to the port and there are some striking *villages perchés* (such as Le Castellet), much favoured by Parisians in particular. From several vantage points on the roads threading across the steep escarpment immediately behind Toulon the views over the naval base and the peninsula of Saint Mandrier are dramatic – notably from Le Gros Cerveau, Mont Caume, Mont Faron and, aptly named for those who wish to make the ascent on foot, the Baou de quatre heures. Further inland, especially in the Morières forest and along the

valley of the Gapeau, several hours' walking will be rewarded with such unspoiled places as the old village of Le Revest, or the delightfully peaceful walled monastery at Montrieux, or with unexpected chapels such as those at Vallaury or Morière-le-Cap. Though there is not the same variety as on the Sainte Baume, this is a region rich in tree and plant life. The same cannot be said for wild animals, however. As in almost every part of Provence (and indeed France as a whole), wildlife has suffered enormously from the national passion for hunting. Signs indicating private reserves (*chasse gardée*) are frequent, and there is something ritualistic in all rural communities about the opening of the hunting season in mid August. Local people will still talk of the 'dialogue' between hunter and beast, claiming that the latter participates 'knowingly', and indeed willingly, in an elaborate game. Areas like the Massif de la Sainte Baume and the Morières forest were once quite well populated with wild boar (*sanglier*); their scarcity today indicates clearly enough who has won.

Two smaller areas in this particular part of Provence, very different in atmosphere from the remote mountains, should also be explored. The first is to the east of Aix and includes Trets and Saint-Maximin (overlooked by the sharp range of hills known as the Mont Aurélien), Brignoles, and the forested country to the north surrounding Barjols and Rians. The second is the coastal strip between Marseille and Toulon, just as popular as the one further east but essentially different in character. Both regions bridge the boundary separating the Bouches-du-Rhône from the Var.

Of the several small, busy market towns in the vicinity of Aix, Trets (pronounced locally as Tress) is all too easily bypassed. Sunk into the surrounding countryside, it appears quite insignificant from a distance, but it is well worth visiting and has deep historical roots. Originally founded by a colony of Greek traders, it later developed as a Gallo-Roman

Twin fountains in Auriol.

town of some importance until it was destroyed by the Saracens. During the Middle Ages it enjoyed renewed prosperity and was linked feudally to Marseille until the very beginning of the eighteenth century. Skirted by the shaded main thoroughfare, the well-preserved old town is still a labyrinth of narrow, vaulted streets with fortified gateways dating from the thirteenth and fourteenth centuries, substantial sectors of the original town walls and the remains of three châteaux. There is also the twelfth-century church of Saint-Victor which contains a splendid example of a barrel-vaulted romanesque roof, as well as some later gothic work and a massive unfinished fifteenth-century belfry.

Trets is well situated as the departure point for a number of relatively small excursions, either north across the upper valley of the Arc towards Sainte Victoire, or into the thickly wooded hills to the south. The roads are quite good, but the well-marked walk to Saint-Zacharie by way of the Oratoire Saint-Jean-du-Puy is especially worthwhile. At a height of over 650 metres the views from this vantage point can be spectacular and on fine days it is possible to see as far as the Alps. It is also possible to explore vast areas of the Aurélian range to the east or the Regagnas to the west on a network of well-tended fire paths. And less than 20 kilometres away to the east is Saint-Maximin.

A place which has attracted pilgrims and tourists alike for centuries, Saint-Maximin sits in a natural gap between the hills, used today by all the major roads in the region. Although basically a nineteenth-century town in design, there is a well-defined medieval area. This is less impressive than the one in Trets, but is benefiting from an increasing amount of con-servationist effort. The town is deservedly known for its magnificent basilica, arguably the finest example of gothic architecture in all Provence and similar to the church at Bourges in the Loire valley much further north. Its position is best appreciated from the northern side of the town, from where it can be seen side-on standing on a very slight hill. Built on the site

---

Ready for Sunday lunch in Saint-Zacharie.

of a sixth-century church, it was begun in the late thirteenth century and was intended as a resting-place for the relics of Mary Magdalene. The reliquary, which contains her skull, can be seen displayed sometimes in the choir and sometimes in the crypt; the church was described in the nineteenth century by the Dominican theologian Lacordaire as 'the third most important tomb in the world after those of Christ and Saint Peter'. Today the visitor is more likely to be impressed by the magnificence of some of its architectural features, and by some of the contents and fittings, and associated buildings.

Although the construction of the basilica lasted for more than four hundred years, there is no belfry, no transepts, and most curiously of all, the west front appears unfinished. Externally the design is also upset by some rather clumsy ornamentation to the apse. Internally, however, the basilica is of massive proportions and balance, a huge, soaring tribute to the Christian faith. And there are baroque details of rich beauty – the multi-coloured marble high altar draped with figures, the carving of the choir-stalls and screen, and the pulpit. Other treasures include the 22 painted wooden panels depicting Christ's passion from the fourteenth and fifteenth centuries, which stand at the eastern end of the north side-aisle. One which shows Christ being presented to Pontius Pilate has the Papal Palace at Avignon as its background. More impressive still is the organ, which dates from the seventeenth century and is one of the best known in France. In 1793 it was saved from destruction by Lucien Bonaparte – the Emperor's brother – who had patriotic music played on it. Opportunities to appreciate its superb tone today are more frequent in July, during the musical evenings organized by the local centre for cultural exchanges.

Adjoining the basilica to the north is the Couvent Royal, originally a Dominican theological school, the earliest part of which also dates from the late thirteenth century. The cloisters and their attendant buildings were occupied by the Dominicans until 1966. Now subject to extensive restoration work, they are the setting for concerts and exhibitions. Yet despite this

emphasis on contemporary culture, one interesting reminder of past religious persecution remains. Two metres or so down from the opening of the well in the cloisters is the entrance to a tunnel through which threatened monks could escape to the forests on the northern flanks of the Sainte Baume.

The road from Saint-Maximin to Rians crosses a fertile plain and then continues through wooded hills cut by narrow valleys, most of which can be explored along well-maintained forest tracks. These woods, which cover the boundary between the departments of the Bouches-du-Rhône and the Var, are a reminder that the latter is the second most wooded *département* in all France. Nevertheless, the villages in this area are numerous and attractive. Rians is a small, peaceful community with some fine houses and fountains. Its continued and not unprosperous existence is due in part to agriculture and wine-making. But like the nearby villages of Artigues, Esparron or Saint-Martin, it has also benefited from an influx of foreigners and Parisians in search of holiday homes, and from the proximity of the nuclear research station at Cadarache.

Many of the villages in this area are quite individual in character, some situated in small depressions surrounded by trees, others poised on outcrops of rock. One of the most impressive is Saint-Martin, where a small community of Scandinavians has settled. The village enjoys a commanding position and its château, much restored in the nineteenth century, probably dates from the twelfth. Externally it is uninspiring, except for a series of grinning and grotesque faces carved into a frieze near the top. Inside, however, it has some notable features, including a huge kitchen, some fine eighteenth-century plaster-work and furniture. The château is privately owned and has been converted into holiday apartments. It is magnificently sited and has one of the finest gardens in the Var, with superb terraces, 300-year-old oaks and large box hedges.

Less than a hundred years ago, many of these

Early morning in Saint-Maximin.

villages were distinguished by specific crafts or small industries. Unfortunately, except as tourist attractions, most have disappeared, though Varages is still noted for pottery, and Rians and Barjols for leatherwork. In Saint-Martin the severed feet of wild goats, hunted in the nearby hills for their hide, can be seen nailed to several doors.

While these communities are lively, colourful places during the spring and summer months, in winter they retreat into themselves. Every four years, however, a festival is held in Barjols which attracts people in their hundreds from far afield. Barjols is the largest of these villages and is known as the Tivoli of Provence on account of its abundant water (there are 22 fountains and 15 public wash-houses). But it is best known for the Fête des Tripettes, held on 16 January.

The story on which this festival is based concerns the remains of St Marcel, who had been Bishop of Die in the Drôme in the fifth century. They were deposited at the monastery of Saint-Maurice, between Aups and Barjols. Eight hundred years later, both villages laid claim to them. The courts in Aix decided that the remains should go to whichever village was nearer, but the villagers of Barjols raided the monastery and stole them before the distances could be measured. It so happened that these events occurred on 16 January 1350, a day when the village traditionally celebrated the ending of a famine long in the past by the providential discovery of an ox. In this ceremony, full of dancing and singing, an ox was blessed, killed and its intestines (*tripettes*) distributed amongst the villagers. With the arrival of the band bearing the remains of St Marcel the two events became intermingled and have remained so ever since.

Today an ox is brought to the church before suffering the same fate as its forebears – though the intestines are no longer distributed! In the evening musicians in the church lead the congregation in the *danse des tripettes* and the following day the beast is roasted in the huge village square, La Rouguière, accompanied by more singing and dancing. This is yet one more example of a Provençal festivity in which pagan and Christian elements are closely interwoven.

Barjols lies in the valley of the Argens, which rises just outside Seillons to the southwest. The countryside around the river is still thickly wooded and in places rises to well over 500 metres. Notable high points include the summit of the Gros Bessillon, whose rocks have been carved by the weather to look like the ruins of some neolithic village, or the hills either side of Châteauvert. Villages worth visiting include Correns, which witnessed a production of Corneille's most famous play, *Le Cid*, in 1667, and Bras, a one-time commandery of the Knights Templar. Each with its own fertile valley and each bypassed by the motorway to Nice, they have remained relatively untouched by tourism. The pools known as the Cours Bénits to the west of Bras should not be missed. It is said that village miscreants used to be cast into these deep waters, while more reliable sources recorded they turned red in 1754 at the time of the great Lisbon earthquake.

By contrast with this area, Brignoles has an altogether different atmosphere. It is a sizeable community (approximately 10,000 inhabitants) and has been the most important town of the region since the Middle Ages, when it was the summer residence for the counts of Provence. Much of its medieval fabric can still be seen, including several gates, narrow streets, the counts' palace, and a house known as the 'maison romane' in the rue des Lanciers, originally used by the counts' military escort. There are also some fine decorated doorways dating from the sixteenth and seventeenth centuries, especially that of the Hôtel Dieu. There is evidence too of much earlier occupation, and the local museum displays one side of a Gallo-Roman sarcophagus that was discovered at the Chapelle-de-la-Gayole 10 kilometres to the west of the town, where the remainder can still be seen. It dates from the third century and is claimed to be the oldest in France.

Like nearby Tourves, Brignoles has owed much of its wealth in recent years to the bauxite industry. Together these places have been responsible for sending nearly three-quarters of the entire French production of bauxite to the aluminium factories at Gardanne and Marseille. As a result Brignoles is evidently prosperous and secure, with smart new suburbs, large hotels, restaurants and cafés, an Olympic-sized swimming complex and an antique fair which attracts dealers from all over France. But there are problems. Local mines are nearing exhaustion and competition from Australia, New Guinea and Greece is severe. As a result unemployment has grown, demonstrations are not unknown, and social and political tension is high, fuelled by the presence of a sizeable immigrant population. No solution has so far emerged and there is an increasing danger of a substantial rift between those who are employed, or who have successfully adapted to a new life based essentially on agriculture and tourism, and those forced into early retirement or redundancy.

The bauxite mines scar the landscape here just as they do north of Marseille, and the red stains on the grass and trees alongside the main roads, especially from the west, can be seen as a symbolic blight on a town that is not entirely certain where it is going. All this is a far cry from the seclusion and tranquillity of those villages sunk in the forests and valleys less than 30 kilometres to the north. But the contrast is significant. In many ways Brignoles presents a microcosm of some of the issues affecting a number of places in the south of France.

The second area worth exploring, the coastal strip between Marseille and Toulon, can be reached by a variety of routes. The quickest and most direct is the one provided by the motorway, the Autoroute de l'Esterel, which links with either Aix or Marseille through Aubagne and from which there are exit points to each of the major resorts. The road has been blasted and hacked through massive crags of pink, grey and pale yellow rock, and some of the views from it are spectacular, especially those over La Ciotat or further east over the bay between Bandol and Sanary. Less practical but a great deal more pleasurable, now that much of the traffic has been syphoned off, are the older

Secluded spots such as this one near Bandol can be reached by the coastal path.

routes to Cassis. That from Marseille runs between the Chaîne de Saint Cyr and the Massif de Puget through the Col de la Gineste; the other leads from Aubagne through Carnoux. The former is breathtakingly dramatic and can be genuinely frightening on a day when the mistral is blowing at its strongest. Despite much improvement during the last ten years, the latter still weaves its way through pine-clad limestone ridges before plunging down towards the sea. Carnoux on this route is an interesting town. It was only created in 1959 and is largely inhabited by French nationals who returned from North Africa just after the Algerian war.

A third and even more rewarding way of making the journey is on foot, by way of the coastal footpath and fire-breaks from either Les Goudes or Callelongue directly south of Marseille. It is also possible to take boat trips from Callelongue to the group of islands just offshore, of which the Ile de Riou is the biggest and the site of important underwater discoveries. In 1952 the explorer Jacques Cousteau retrieved three earthenware cups from the sea here which were subsequently dated to 2000 BC. Further underwater expeditions produced 3000 wine jars and 6000 pieces of crockery, the cargo of a boat destined for Delos. This part of the coast is particularly dangerous and it is thought that the remains of other ancient wrecks may still be discovered.

The land rises abruptly from the sea here, forming some of the highest cliffs in France. (La Grande Tête between Cassis and La Ciotat reaches nearly 400 metres.) The scenery is some of the most inhospitable of the entire French Mediterranean coast – a jumble of peaks and twisted crags, scored by deep valleys and so eroded by the wind and salt that the limestone has been polished to a brilliant white finish. The *calanques* are also to be found here – deep, sheltered creeks which continue the inland valleys along fault lines and which resemble minute Norwegian fjords. Impressively beautiful, they have been the centre of

much controversy. In 1913 one of them, Port-Miou, was scandalously allowed to be developed as a quarry and building material is still taken from it to be used in Cassis. Several can be reached by surfaced roads and fire paths are used illegitimately to reach others by car. As a result small huts (*cabanons*) have been built without any main services and, more alarmingly, planning permission has been given for the erection of more substantial dwellings. The consequences for the natural beauty of the area are obvious, and since the mid 1970s a society has been established in order to protect it. This seems to have been largely successful, a notable landmark being the reforestation of a substantial area in 1975 in which over a thousand people were involved. Nevertheless, unless the area is declared a protected natural region, like parts of the Camargue or the Ile de Port-Cros off the coast at Hyères, its special character is likely to disappear completely.

Today it is still possible to enjoy the *calanques*. The principal ones can be visited as part of boat tours from Cassis and La Ciotat, but others, such as the Calanques de Mounine or de Sugiton, can only be reached on foot by way of paths which demand considerable effort and stamina. Much of this terrain is in fact so testing that even the most experienced mountaineers use it as a favourite training area. The sea itself is 25 or 30 metres deep in places, and though it is very cold, it attracts many who enjoy underwater fishing. But there are virtually no beaches and the hundreds of tiny, rocky inlets remain inaccessible except to those with small boats and sufficient skill to navigate between the rocks.

Of the resorts, the first and arguably the prettiest is Cassis. Squeezed between the cliffs, a long, narrow harbour is overlooked by bright, attractively maintained houses and cafés. Frantically busy at the height of summer, it is rather like a less fashionable version of Saint-Tropez and is certainly far less pretentious – and less expensive. Small boats come and go, fishermen mend their nets and sell their catch in the early morning, local youths weave through the crowds of sun-drenched tourists on their powered bicycles and

Sanary-sur-Mer.

131

the clink and clatter of *boules* is almost constant. During the rest of the year Cassis is much quieter and re-emerges as a genuine fishing port, but its protected site ensures a climate mild enough to continue to attract people from Marseille and its hinterland.

Unlike the much larger La Ciotat a dozen or so kilometres away across the headland of the Montagne de la Canaille, Cassis bears relatively few traces of its past, though it is known that there was a settlement here before the arrival of the Romans. A fourteenth-century château overlooks the village from high on the cliffs to the east, but it has been much restored. Similarly, although the original street plan can still be seen, the medieval part of the town was rebuilt in the eighteenth century. In the last few decades Cassis has become much more prosperous. Its population is multiplied several times during July and August and the attempt to accommodate as many visitors as possible has inevitably resulted in a rash of holiday apartment blocks, but mercifully the local terrain does not permit overmuch development of this kind. The fashionable new houses set amongst pine trees, which enjoy magnificent views over the old streets of the village 100 metres or so below, are considerably more acceptable. More than most of the places along this part of the coast, Cassis has succeeded in remaining relatively unspoilt.

There are two main routes from Cassis to La Ciotat. The first runs parallel to the motorway and approaches the town from the north, descending steeply from the Couronne de Charlemagne. The second follows the clifftop to the point known as the Sémaphore, from which there are extensive views along the coast in both directions and back inland to the Sainte Baume. Well protected by hills to the north, the Baie de la Ciotat is very slightly pincer-shaped. On the Cap de l'Aigle on the western point, a series of rust-coloured, shell-shaped cliffs thrust up by a massive land movement look as though they could have been a source of inspiration for the Sydney Opera House. And just out to sea is their geological extension, the Ile Verte, a rocky, tree-covered island which can be easily reached by boat. On the other side of the bay, the Pointe Fauconnière juts aggressively into the sea. According to one version of a legend, the ancient submerged city of Tauroentum lies on this side of the bay. The bells can still be heard on some nights and the city is haunted by a massive bull who is said to come ashore to feed off local grapes in the late summer and autumn. (Another version places Tauroentum further east along the bay between the mainland and the Ile des Embiez at Le Brusc.)

The main town of La Ciotat runs north-south down the western side of the bay. Originally a Greek settlement (Kitharista), it had a chequered history for several hundred years before emerging in the sixteenth century as an important port involved with the increasing Mediterranean trade with the East. Some interesting houses dating from the seventeenth and eighteenth centuries can be seen in the narrow streets running down to the harbour. A church from the same period, Notre-Dame-de-l'Assomption, contains a striking painting of the *Descent from the Cross* by the Belgian artist Louis Finson – known as Finsonius. (Some of his other works can be seen in the church of Saint-Jean-de-Malte at Aix and in the Aubanel museum at Avignon.)

In the nineteenth century the poet Lamartine was moved to define La Ciotat as a perfect blend of 'charm and strength'. Within a short time this strength was manifested in a flourishing ship-building industry which still dominates the older part of the town. The docks, where huge container ships are built and repaired, provide work for over 6000 people, creating an economic and social climate that is noticeably different from places such as Brignoles. Many of the dock workers are housed in two interesting and contrasting conglomerations of buildings. The first, in traditional Provençal style, is just over a hundred years old; the second, built in the early 1970s, is a series of white geometric blocks with colourful terraces and small gardens.

Although always visible, these shipyards are soon

The spectacular site of Cassis.

forgotten once the coast begins to turn east along the base of the bay. A vast marina with boats stacked in specially-designed racks leads to a series of beaches extending away to Les Lecques and La Madrague. These beaches have been made with care; stone breakwaters have been erected to counteract erosion and the natural rocks have been covered by hundreds of tonnes of very fine gravel. This is the centre of La Ciotat's other principal source of income, and there is a somewhat strange clash between the holiday flats, *le fastfood* and *le snack* and the existence of a medical centre, specializing in salt-water treatment. By contrast, the beaches of Les Lecques are of fine sand. Smaller than La Ciotat, but just as colourful and popular, Les Lecques' original status as a resort can be judged from the magnificent old hotels in the village, and it is especially popular with families and *colonies de vacances*. Unfortunately ease of access and a workable terrain have encouraged the construction of several long apartment blocks in the less than appropriately named Baie des Anges which extends southward from here. Although separated from Les Lecques and its beaches by a major road, these blocks none the less threaten to overpower what charm this coastal strip still possesses.

Fortunately the hinterland remains attractive. Saint-Cyr, for example, still has a freshness and individuality that are relatively unspoiled. Various excursions are possible from this colourful little village, either by car or on foot – to the sea, inland to La Cadière (preserved as a 'true' Provençal village) or across the headland to Bandol. Just north of Saint-Cyr, by the side of the link-road to the motorway, a pair of vineyards is entirely enclosed by extraordinarily massive dry-stone walls 2 or 3 metres wide and almost as high. To the south is the restored thirteenth-century Château de Baumelles, now one of the many local wine estates and to be compared, for example, with the Château des Pradeaux at La Ciotat or the Mas de Fontblanche on the road from Carnoux to Cassis. And on the coast only 5 kilometres

---

Terracing behind La Ciotat.

away is the Calanque du Port d'Alon, with its century-old pine trees. The Baie de la Motte is also easily accessible and the coastal path from here leads either back to La Madrague or east to Bandol.

The coastal scenery here is less harsh than that west of Cassis, but in many places it is almost as inaccessible. Some building has been allowed on the flatter clifftops, often, as at Le Déffend, strikingly modern in design, protected by remote-controlled gates and well hidden by the thick covering of oaks and pines. Spared the forest fires which have ravaged so much of Provence in recent years, these clifftops are also rich in local herbs and flowers – thyme, rosemary, laurels, violets and wild roses – and are best visited in early spring.

Those who walk the few kilometres to the next bay, the Baie de Bandol, experience a complete change in atmosphere. Protected from the north by a semicircle of hills and facing directly south, Bandol enjoys a climate which fully justifies its reputation as an all-year resort. With its long promenade, sandy beaches, palm, mimosa and eucalyptus trees, it is self-evidently much more fashionable than Cassis or La Ciotat. Yet it is a much more recent town, having only developed into a community of any size about two hundred years ago. In the nineteenth century Bandol was a port for the exportation of wine, but once seaside holidays became fashionable, it attracted increasing numbers of visitors. The writer Katherine Mansfield lived here and Winston Churchill returned regularly before World War 2. The magnificent hotel in which he used to stay towards the eastern end of the town is now divided into privately owned flats, but it still manages to convey the flavour of a period now submerged by one that is more brash and materialistic.

The values of the late twentieth century are particularly well demonstrated by the Ile de Bendor, only a few minutes by boat from Bandol and a deserted rock until 1950. Since then, together with the Ile des Embiez to the south, it has been developed by Paul Ricard, the *pastis* magnate, into a tourist attraction. Bendor offers its visitors an imitation Provençal fishing port and village, a zoo, and three museums, one containing relics from Greek and Roman settlements in

the bay, one devoted to the sea, and the third containing an extraordinary collection of over 6000 bottles from three dozen different countries.

For those who are not interested in such attractions, or in a holiday entirely devoted to the sea and beach in summer, the large promontory of Cap Sicié between Six-Fours and Toulon is worth exploring. The southern half of this promontory, overlooked from the north by the Gros Cerveau just 15 kilometres away, is thickly wooded by the Forêt de Janas. Although some attempts have been made to attract tourists here – a zoo, tennis courts and a physical fitness course – it is possible to get away even in July and August. At the ruined look-out tower of Notre Dame du Mai, the southernmost cliffs rise to over 350 metres. There are also winding cliff-paths to explore, which at one turn will reveal glaringly white limestone rock faces and at another thick vegetation. These cliffs continue up the east side of the Cap to the tiny village of Fabregas, noted for its grey sand which is used in the treatment of rheumatism. And only a few kilometres further north is Les Sablettes, where it is possible to take an attractive boat trip to Toulon or to cross by the causeway onto the peninsula of Saint-Mandrier-sur-Mer.

Inland, further north and virtually central to the Cap, are the remains of the old *village perché* of Six-Fours, abandoned and eventually demolished in the nineteenth century to allow for the construction of a fort. There is still a spectacular view over Toulon, but little remains of the original village buildings. For a small but interesting example of what the village must have been like, however, it is only necessary to walk 2 kilometres north to the beautifully simple sixth-century church of Notre-Dame-de-Pépiole. Like so many similar areas along this strip of coast, Cap Sicié is best explored in the spring when the forests are at their most attractive, when there are fewer people about and when the small villages by the sea recapture something of their true nature. In winter it can be bleak, but even so it provides an interesting contrast to Marseille or Aix, both only thirty minutes away down the motorway. Beyond Toulon and Hyères to the east the coast changes in both character and atmosphere. Inland the Var is seen for kilometre upon kilometre at its superb best.

Fruit market in Bandol.

Moustiers-Ste-Marie

Séillans
Vérignon
Bargemon
Fayence
Aups
Montferrat
Callas
Ampus
Villecroze
Tourtour
St-Paul-en-Forêt
Barjols
Salernes
Bagnols-en-Forêt
Cotignac
Draguignan
Carcès
Le Muy
Argens
St-Raphaël
Le Thoronet
Couloubrier
Fréjus
Le Vieux-Cannet
Brignoles
Le Cannet-des-Maures
Le Luc
Les Issambres
Ste-
Maxime
La Garde-Freinet
Port
Grimaud
St-Tropez
Massif des Maures
Grimaud
Marseille
Collobrières
Cogolin
Gassin
Gapeau
Cuers
Pierrefeu-du-Var
Ramatuelle
Cassis
Cavalaire-sur-Mer
La Ciotat
Solliès-Pont
Cavalière
Pramousquier
Bandol
Bormes-les-Mimosas
Toulon
Le Lavandou
Le Pradet
Hyères
Carqueiranne
L'Almanarre
Iles d'Hyères
Héliopolis
Ile du Levant
Ile de
Bagaud
Giens
Ile de
Porquerolles
Ile de Port-Cros

M e d i t e r r a n e a n

4
Toulon and Beyond

Toulon – Hyères – Cavalaire-sur-Mer – Saint-Tropez – Sainte-Maxime – Fréjus – Massif des Maures – Collobrières – Fayence – Draguignan – Aups – Le Luc

For many French people Toulon and the navy are synonymous. '*Toulon, c'est la Marine*' has become an accepted colloquialism and, like most expressions of its kind, is rooted in some degree of truth. There is evidence that Toulon served as a port as long ago as the fourth century and Louis XII used it to launch his fleet in his wars against Italy 1200 years later. But Toulon's importance really dates from the seventeenth century, when Louis XIV instructed his principal military engineer, Sébastien Vauban, to develop it as a major naval base. Vauban's work on what he described (in a much-quoted phrase) as 'the finest and safest port in the Mediterranean' can still be seen in the vast dock known as the *darse vieille*, now one of three.

Since then and despite a dramatic set-back in 1720, when 17,000 out of a total population of 26,000 are said to have died from the plague, Toulon has continued to grow. At the time of the Revolution it was, like Marseille, staunchly royalist. The republican victory was eventually assured in 1793 by a young junior officer, Napoleon Bonaparte. In subsequent years, Napoleon was to use the port as his base for colonial expeditions. In the first half of the twentieth century Toulon developed into the principal 'war port' of France, both in terms of national defence and in terms of its ship-building facilities. When the Germans invaded the south of France in 1942, the fleet stationed at Toulon was, with the exception of a few submarines, deliberately sunk on orders from the Vichy government.

Since that disaster, however, Toulon's naval importance has continued to evolve. With the possible exception of Bordeaux and its wine trade, no other town in France has been so totally preoccupied by its principal activity. The population of greater Toulon is now about 350,000, of whom 30,000 are connected in some way with the sea. Yet this evolution is not without problems. New technology has brought the usual attendant threat of redundancy, land-based engineers are growing in number by contrast with sailors, and despite successful links with the shipyards in La Ciotat, the future of the entire complex seems to be uncertain. There is also a political division between, on the one hand, a conservative element made up of retired officers and new management personnel introduced largely from Brittany, and, on the other, a hardening militant core of dock workers. And between all these groups and the civilian population, known as *les moccos*, there is often a good deal of tension, if not open friction. The problems are still a long way from becoming as acute as they are in Marseille, but the danger signs are there.

It is easy to understand why Vauban reacted to Toulon as he did. The principal bay, or Petite Rade, is

Spécialités de la région.

---

approached through an opening barely 2 kilometres wide and largely blocked by a sea wall. From here the coast sweeps around to Le Pradet to the east, forming the larger bay known as the Grande Rade, which is overlooked by two vantage points, the Cap Cépet and La Pointe de Carqueiranne. Inland, the port is sheltered by limestone hills, rising to over 500 metres, which fold round to form a natural amphitheatre and provide protection against the mistral. (Historically, they deterred invaders as well.) One result, as at Cassis, is an equable climate which has led to an increase in tourism and in particular in holiday sea-traffic. At the suburb of Le Mourillon alone, for example, there is now mooring space for over a thousand boats. But such natural advantages do not always bring benefits. Because of the terrain, rail and in particular road communications have had to be squeezed through the very centre of the town. At present, therefore, the motorway from east and west ends abruptly, and only a massive engineering feat – like the tunnel beneath Lyon – could resolve the inevitable traffic congestion in the centre of the city.

The old town, or Basse Ville, has been largely pedestrianized and still has much of its medieval character. But, as in Marseille, there is also a high proportion of squalid and dilapidated dwellings which are mostly inhabited by North Africans or Spaniards. Restoration is well in hand, but this area contrasts sharply with the expensive apartment blocks of Super Toulon on the north side of the city, and with occasional refurbishments or individual new buildings. The Caisse d'Epargne, for example, is an interesting futuristic conception constructed almost entirely from aluminium and glass.

Toulon was severely bombed in World War 2 – eight times in all – but too much of the rebuilding has been unimaginative. Fortunately a number of historic buildings did survive and others have been thoughtfully restored. These include the cathedral of Sainte-Marie-Majeure – originally known as Notre-Dame-de-la-Seds – where a grandiose seventeenth-century façade mixes rather uncomfortably with thirteenth-century romanesque architecture and with later nineteenth-century modifications. The churches of Saint-Louis and Saint-François-de-Paule have also been restored; both were badly damaged but have now been made good. The latter, in the square Louis Blanc, resembles a number of churches to be found in Nice and contains some fine seventeenth-century wood carving – a gilt statue of the Virgin, the altar and pulpit.

The art museum too is well worth visiting. Its celebrated caryatids by Pierre Puget, La Force and La Fatigue were so much admired by Louis XIV that he nearly removed them to Paris, and the museum also contains a fine collection of French, Italian and Flemish painting from the sixteenth and seventeenth centuries

---

The elaborate war memorial that fronts the Grand Hôtel in Toulon.

and of local work. The naval museum is equally interesting and important, with displays of original documents, maps and scale models of ships across the ages. The hard-labour prison, La Bagne, can also be visited. This once housed Victor Hugo's famous character Jean Valjean, and also François Vidocq, the arch-criminal turned policeman on whom Balzac based the demonic Vautrin in *Le Père Goriot*. And if the atmosphere here is too oppressive, the circus performers' festival in July and August, or the Salon Nautique in May, will redress the balance. The twentieth-century writer François Mauriac once described Toulon – not without some exaggeration perhaps – as the 'most Shakespearian' of all French towns.

Only a dozen kilometres from the bustle, noise and dirt of Toulon is the town which, until Louis XIV's intervention, enjoyed greater prestige. Hyères owed that prestige to salt, and it was once linked in its trading activities with the salt-producing area to the west of Marseille. The town's name derives from the Provençal *ièro* or *aire*, which has come to mean zone or area (or motorway lay-by) in modern French. Today Hyères can be approached from Toulon either by way of La Crau across the plain drained by the Gapeau and its tributaries, or along the coast through Le Pradet and Carqueiranne. The second route is by far the more rewarding. Despite the encroachment of increasingly expensive residential development, the hills of La Colle Noire, Paradis and Le Mont des Oiseaux, with their vines, pine trees and luxuriant gardens, are still attractive. There are numerous look-out points, the coastal path known as the *sentier des douaniers* leads to some delightful views, and along the esplanade at Carqueiranne itself there are some of the most enormous pine trees in this part of France.

Remains of Greek settlements and evidence of a Roman colony have been unearthed at Hyères and also at L'Almanarre on the coast to the south. In later years, Hyères became a port of embarkation for the Crusades (St Louis sailed from here in 1254). In the sixteenth century Catherine de Medici considered building a villa here because of the equable climate, and this natural advantage was to be the basis of Hyères' later prosperity. It is the oldest tourist resort on the Riviera and has been particularly popular with the English. Queen Victoria used to visit it regularly and so did Robert Louis Stevenson. For a century from around 1820 the town's popularity was seriously challenged only by Nice, which eventually became more fashionable. Between the two world wars its reputation declined, but it began to pick up again rapidly in the 1950s and is now once again a mecca for holiday-makers.

Built into the southern face of Les Maurettes, an outcrop of the superb Massif des Maures to the north, the old town is most attractive. Parts of the fortifications and the original château can be seen on the north side, and the centre is a well-preserved medieval complex with some especially fine doors and windows and curious locking lintels. The principal suburbs which developed around the turn of the century also have a special charm. Although now rather seedy, the imposing detached houses set in substantial gardens with palm trees much in evidence create a distinctly colonial atmosphere and it is easy to see why Hyères appealed to the English.

Beyond the town, however, some of the immediate surroundings are far less agreeable and have led to serious pollution problems. To the southeast there is a large, swampy area where the aerodrome is situated and further south again, towards the Giens peninsula, there are extensive salt flats. As around Fos or at the mouth of the Argens near Fréjus, the combination has proved damaging, and exhaust fumes from regular and enormous traffic jams along the peninsular road have also taken their toll. Fortunately the town has not been inactive. In 1972 nearly 5 kilometres of beach were closed and cleaned, and strenuous attempts were made to reduce the polluting agents. The campaign was successful, but there is now another threat. With the salt industry in decline, permission is being sought to develop the Salins and Etang des Pesquiers into a huge

Dormant boats in winter at Hyères.

Provençal spider plant at Giens.

tourist complex. Even with careful planning such a project would be disastrous. Giens itself, already a site for *tourisme de luxe*, would almost certainly be swamped, and the restrictions on the development of the off-shore islands, the Iles d'Hyères, might also be re-examined.

This group of islands – to which Giens also once belonged – is one of Provence's most attractive features. Known certainly since the sixteenth century as the Golden Isles, the Iles d'Or, they were the haunt of smugglers and pirates for centuries; they have been bitterly disputed in war and have been used as religious retreats. Today they are besieged by tourists, though one, the Ile du Levant, is almost entirely occupied by a military missile base and access is forbidden (except to the naturist colony of Héliopolis on the western tip). The largest, Porquerolles, where it is possible to stay, has belonged to the State since 1971. At the time the island was purchased a private

company was planning an initial development of 2500 apartments and chalets, but no further tourist facilities have been allowed. Cars are banned, though cycles can be hired by those who prefer not to walk. Port-Cros and Bagaud (which is uninhabited), and a surrounding belt of sea 600 metres wide have been designated as a national park since 1963. Port-Cros, the most rocky of the islands, especially to the south, is almost entirely wooded (pines and green oaks), and all kinds of wild plants and birds survive here which are no longer found on the mainland. There are numerous beautiful walks, especially to the Vallon de Solitude to the south.

The measures to protect the islands came only just in time. Such was the degree of pollution that they were in danger of becoming sterile and even now the situation will have to be carefully monitored. The example of what has been allowed to happen to the *calanques* should be a warning. Hundreds of tourists, arriving from various coastal ports in seemingly flimsy boats, inevitably cause some damage, however strictly controlled, as do the military activities on the Ile du Levant. For the visitor the Iles d'Hyères *are* beautiful and impossible to resist. The sea is clear, the sand fine. Even at the height of the summer season a walk of twenty minutes or so will lead to a beach edged with pines that is quite likely to be deserted. In the autumn and winter, when access by boat from the mainland is more limited, the islands offer hours of genuine (if temporary) escape.

To the east of Hyères lies the stretch of coast which was 'discovered' and developed as a new Riviera during the inter-war years. Inland is the range of hills known as the Massif des Maures, 15 or 20 kilometres wide in places and densely forested. This area stretching east and north to Saint-Tropez, Sainte-Maxime and Saint-Raphaël accommodates the biggest proportion of the two million or so tourists who find their way to the Var each year. Since about 1960 the growth in holiday homes, apartment blocks, hotels and

Saint-Clair, where the hills of the Massif des Maures come down to the very shore.

camp-sites has been enormous. There are few more telling contrasts than between the expensive but tasteful residential developments on the east side of the Cap Bénat promontory and the complex of breeze-block and concrete boxes in Le Lavandou. Similarly, Cavalaire-sur-Mer to the east has expanded almost as far as the steep slopes of the hills of Les Pradels beneath which it shelters.

Yet, busy and congested as this length of the coast is in summer, it is always possible to find tiny deserted creeks, just as they still exist between La Ciotat and Bandol. Moreover, once September arrives, the tourists depart and the shutters of the *résidences secondaires* are closed. During the rest of the year life returns to normal and the individuality of these villages reappears. They are linked by the *corniche* or coast road which winds across the face of the steep southern slopes of the Massif where it plunges into the sea. The views are tremendous; only those from the coastal path, the *chemin des douaniers*, are more exciting. In spring the bay trees, eucalyptus, pines and cork oaks on the hills are coloured by patches of yellow mimosas and wild roses, while a bright violet flower known as the sea fig grows abundantly near the edge of the sea. Unfortunately a heavy and late frost in 1985 severely 'burned' or killed many of the more exotic trees and plants. Mimosas suffered particularly, while hundreds of palms were reduced to severely pollarded stumps in an attempt to save them.

Originally most of these small resorts relied on fishing for their livelihood. The tunny was the most profitable catch, fished with a huge and elaborate system of nets known as the *madrague*, or, in Provençal, *tonnaio*. The nets had three compartments of diminishing size which were designed to allow the small fish, on which the tunny fed, to escape, while trapping the bigger ones. In 1603, Henri IV unwisely granted exclusive fishing rights to one Antoine Boyer, and the Boyer family continued to enjoy this privilege for three centuries. Their *madragues* – seven in all between Toulon and Saint-Tropez – were so effective that the supply of fish was eventually exhausted and has never really recovered. Local tunny is still more expensive than that imported from abroad. But fishing on a more modest scale continues. Saint-Clair, Cavalière, the exceptionally pretty village of Pramous-quier and Cavalaire all have their fleets of boats and, as in Cassis, the opportunity to buy from the morning's catch should not be missed, even though prices are high.

From Cavalaire-sur-Mer the main road runs due north to Port Grimaud across the base of the Camarat peninsula. With Saint-Tropez as its principal resort, this has become one of France's most sought after coastal regions. Even so, such is the nature of the terrain that many unspoiled rocky inlets and tiny islands can still be discovered. The path known as the *sentier du Gigaro* which leads along the southern coast to the Cap Lardier and round into the Baie de la Briande provides access to some. Elsewhere, however, especially along the fine sandy beaches to the east, private luxury developments have appeared, most notably those at Pampelonne and the Plage de Tahiti. And there is Saint-Tropez itself.

Few villages in France have enjoyed such a rise to fame and fortune. The nineteenth-century writer Guy de Maupassant described Saint-Tropez in one of his short stories, 'Sur l'eau', as 'one of those modest towns which has emerged from the sea like a shell, nourished by fish and sea-air'. Nearly a hundred years later a French social and economic historian referred to it rather more prosaically as a place where 'millionaires, stars, snobs and hippies gather in a dense and colourful crowd'. During July and August the truth of this is only too apparent. In this period Saint-Tropez receives, on average, eight to ten thousand cars per day, while an unofficial figure of 50,000 visitors was given for an August Sunday in the mid 1980s. The port can be packed with boats of all sizes, shapes, descriptions and nationalities. This is not just one of the playgrounds of France, but of the world.

Yet Saint-Tropez has no real beach of its own, faces north, has an inadequate road system and not enough

Avenue of palms at Cavalière.

146

hotels. The growth of its reputation and popularity has been due almost entirely to various people who have been associated with it and who have promoted it: writers such as Jean Cocteau, Emile Verhaeran, Colette and Françoise Sagan; painters such as Utrillo, Matisse, Dufy, Bonnard and Braque; the music-hall actress Mistinguett and, since the 1950s in particular, film stars (of whom Brigitte Bardot is perhaps the best known). For Colette, who spent much of her life between 1923 and 1936 just outside Salins to the east of Saint-Tropez, no place could be more beautiful. According to her the quality of the blue light here was only found elsewhere in dreams – the sort of thing Cézanne said about Aix.

Out of season, Saint-Tropez resembles a ghost village. Officially over 6000 people are meant to live here permanently – just 2000 more than in 1920 – but it seems far fewer. Cafés are closed; the vast municipal car-park and the marina are nearly empty. If you can, this is the time to explore the network of narrow streets, climb up to the sixteenth-century fortress or visit the town's art gallery, whose superb collection contains many works by painters who have lived in Saint-Tropez.

The town's history is commemorated on two occasions in May and June by festivals known locally as *bravades*. Having been destroyed by the Saracens, Saint-Tropez was revived in the fifteenth century by a group of Genoese families who were allowed to settle there and rebuild it in 1470: in recognition of their efforts they paid no taxes. In 1637 during the Wars of Religion they defeated a Spanish fleet which was threatening this stretch of coastline. Presumably worried by this display of military and naval strength, Louis XIV's gesture of thanks was to remove all their privileges at once! The victory, however, is still celebrated on 15 June. A month earlier, between 16 and 18 May, the Fête de Saint-Tropez is a much more colourful and noisy affair.

Saint-Tropez, serene before the summer invasion.

The most popular belief concerning the saint is that he was a converted Roman soldier from Pisa called Torpes, who was executed in AD 68 for failing to renounce his new Christian faith. His body, together with a dog and a cockerel, was set adrift in an open boat, which eventually came to shore near the site of the present town. A rich widow from Cavalaire, who had already had a premonition of the whole event in a dream, took the body and secretly buried it. (The similarity with certain aspects of the legend of Saintes-Maries-de-la-Mer is noticeable.) For the last four hundred years a coloured and ornate wooden bust of the saint, with moustaches and staring, surprised eyes, has been carried from the church to the Chapel of Sainte-Anne. The whole affair is boisterous and noisy. The participants, the *bravadaires*, are dressed in military and naval uniform and fire salvos of muskets as they walk through the streets. Not surprisingly the celebrations usually continue long into the night with fire-crackers and dancing. For the citizens of Saint-Tropez the *fête* is a wholly serious matter and not a tourist attraction; while it does inevitably draw people from elsewhere it is very much a local affair. Another version of the story is that the saint's head was originally an effigy from the prow of a boat, and that Tropez derives from *trovato* or 'found'. Not surprisingly, this account is less welcome!

The growth of Saint-Tropez has affected much of the peninsula, partly simply as a result of the seasonal influx of people, partly more permanently. The principal *villages perchés* of Ramatuelle and Gassin revert to something like their true characters only during the winter and spring. From Gassin's long north-facing terrace, the sight of early-morning mist in winter or spring hanging in the trees below, with a thin wreath of smoke rising from some hidden *cabanon* or *bastide*, seems light-years away from the bustle and noise of Saint-Tropez in summer. But although they are still attractive, Ramatuelle and Gassin can never revert to being the peasant communities they were only a couple of generations ago. As a walk through the walled cemeteries will quickly reveal, few of the original families are left. And further changes may be

149

Left The place de l'Ormeau, Saint-Tropez, throngs with people during the summer months. Closed shutters indicate houses abandoned for the winter.

Above Autumnal sun on Ramatuelle.

151

on the way. The seasonal imbalance of population in this whole area is so great that plans exist to create an entirely new village designed by François Spoerry, the architect of Port Grimaud. The few remaining local people not surprisingly see this as a further strain on the natural resources of their region and as an invitation to speculators to push up the price of land and property even further. Unless such plans are dropped or central government intervenes to protect the area, however, the future as far as the local people are concerned does not look encouraging.

For the less sceptical, Port Grimaud is an example of what can be achieved if new developments are well planned. Five kilometres from Grimaud itself, it lies at the edge of the plain formed from silt deposits at the end of the Golfe de Saint Tropez. It was begun in 1964 and is the most famous example of what the French call a *cité lacustre* – but here a sea- rather than a lake-side community. Spoerry intended to create an imitation Provençal village, though the result is more like a mini-Venice. Houses are built on long platforms; each can be reached by boat and the whole complex is rather like a huge marina. Visitors are not allowed to take their cars into the village. Responses to Port Grimaud have been mixed. Soon after the completion of the first stage one critic derided it as a 'Mediterranean Disneyland'! But in general it has to be considered a success, both in its own right and also because it has removed some of the immediate pressure from Saint-Tropez.

The original Roman port of Grimaud inland (some of the mooring posts can still be seen) and the attractive village of Cogolin next to it are both worth visiting. Although they are both popular as resorts, the villagers of Cogolin in particular still practise many traditional activities – making cane furniture, reeds for musical instruments, corks and the knotted-pile wool carpets unique in France. By encouraging tourists to take guided tours of the factories, the two principal sources of income have successfully been brought together. Cogolin also has a claim to an important place

in more recent history. Colonel de Lattre set up his headquarters here in August 1944 from where he directed allied operations in what became known as the Battle of Provence. His victory is commemorated in Cogolin as elsewhere by the rue de Lattre.

Once beyond Port Grimaud at the base of the bay, the coast road runs northeast, passing through another sequence of small, well-tended villages. This coast too is protected from the north by wooded hills rising in places to over 300 metres. There are fine views in both directions from several points along the road – in particular from the Cap des Sardinaux, just beyond Sainte-Maxime, and from the Pointe des Issambres. Many of the properties in this area are imaginatively and attractively designed and have been built at considerable expense; unlike those on the Saint-Tropez peninsula they do not have a hinterland crossed by main roads. Although access to the vast Forêt communale des Arcs some 10 kilometres inland is simple enough, there are only two roads which cross the Massif, the main one being from Sainte-Maxime to Le Muy, 20 kilometres to the north. This whole coastline is best explored at leisure, ideally in spring before its superb array of wild flowers has been affected by the heat or, worse, by the pollution from the daily influx of several thousand cars.

A third of the way along towards Fréjus is Sainte-Maxime, built where the Préconil flows into the sea and considered by many to be the most attractive of the resorts. With its south-facing bay and marina providing a perfect sun-trap, its position is certainly better than that of Saint-Tropez, though even in summer stiff, fresh breezes from the north can blow disconcertingly down the river valley. On the other hand, this valley provides immediate access to the wooded hinterland of the Massif des Maures which, within 5 kilometres, rises to more than 500 metres.

Vestiges of Sainte-Maxime's past can still be seen. Roman baths have been preserved near La Nartelle on the north side while a granite menhir just inland, known as La Mère, is a witness to an even more ancient culture. Attractions from more recent times include a late fifteenth-century château (now the town hall) and

Port Grimaud: a modern-day Venice.

153

the principal church. This contains a splendid altar carved in Provençal marble which originated from the Chartreuse de la Verne near Collobrières (see p. 160). But since the 1950s Sainte-Maxime has been substantially redesigned by the architect Ricardo Boffil. The result is a town-scape of clean, unfussy lines accentuated by pastel colours and white plaster-work. Unlike Saint-Tropez, which even out of season can seem tight and self-contained (like many a true Provençal village), Sainte-Maxime is open and bright. It is a fast-growing resort. Its casino is one of the most popular on the coast, and it has proportionately more festivals than any other town in the area. The Fête des Mimosas on the last Sunday in May even rivals the flower festivals of Nice.

The simplest route from Sainte-Maxime to Fréjus is by way of the coast, around the gentle sweep of the Baie de Bougnon and through Les Issambres. An alternative and just as attractive route runs directly north from the tiny resort of La Garonnette through the Col de Bougnon. It then follows the contours of the hills emerging into the fertile valley of the Argens just 4 kilometres west of Fréjus.

Fréjus was founded by Julius Caesar as a trading centre in the first century BC. It was known as Forum Julii and quickly developed in importance, becoming second port in the entire Empire (after Ostia) and the most famous Roman city in the south of France after Arles. Before long it had become a major market town and vital check-point on the Via Aurelia (a small paved section of which still exists). At its height it had a population of about 25,000, and the size of the settlement is reflected in extensive Roman remains, the oldest and the most complete in France. They are not as fine as those in Arles or Vaison, but they are found almost at every turn. Excavations were pursued in earnest in the 1920s and 1930s and it is known that still more remains lie buried beneath the railway line. (A popular French expression says that you only have to take up a flagstone in Fréjus to find a Roman underneath.)

Of the buildings that can now be seen, the theatre (which is still used) and the arena are the best known.

The latter once accommodated 12,000 spectators and is famous for its elliptical shape and for the rare, greenish stone in which it is built. In recent years, however, it has been turned into a Luna Park, sorely undermining its dignity. The delightful mosaic called the Combat des Coqs is a small-scale reminder of Roman art which should not be missed. It is to be found in the listed building known as the Propriété des Pelloux-Gervais.

Fréjus owed its early importance to its position on the coast and its decline began as the port gradually silted up. Revenue from the export of salt, corn and marble stopped. Despite a flourishing medieval religious community, the town could offer little or nothing to encourage commercial growth and by the eighteenth century its population had fallen to 2000. It was to remain at this level until the early twentieth century, when Fréjus was chosen as a centre for colonial troops from North Africa and the Far East who fought in World War I. Two military camps and graveyards to the north of the town are reminders of this period. One, the Camp de Caïs, has a sadly neglected concrete reproduction of the Missiri mosque at Djenné in the Sudan; and there is a Buddhist temple on the N7 to Cannes, just outside the Camp de Gallieni. The temple is still used for worship and the slope leading to it is an extraordinary and incongruous display of all kinds of animals and reptiles made out of stucco. The area has also been designated as the burial ground for the remains of soldiers who fought in the Korean War and which are to be brought back to France in the late 1980s.

In the years immediately after World War I the population rose rapidly (to 20,000 in 1920), and with the development of tourism Fréjus was reborn. Today it is easily the biggest town between Toulon and Cannes, with a permanent population of nearly 35,000 and far more during the summer months. And it is still growing. In the mid 1980s, for example, the government launched a scheme for the development of another 10,000 state-subsidized apartments here. As

Panels on the cathedral door at Fréjus.

154

with other places along this coast, the town's size and position are beginning to cause problems. Fréjus is now over a kilometre from the sea, while the principal holiday beaches are those along the coast adjoining Saint-Raphaël. This means that people arriving from inland have to pass by or through the town to get to them. Traffic congestion can be some of the worst in this part of France, particularly on the roads from the northwest leading from the junction of the N7 and the Provençal motorway. And the situation is aggravated by the amount of traffic generated by local light industry and by the naval air base to the south. The base is built on reclaimed land at the mouth of the Argens. Barred to the general public, it is screened by a hedge of reeds and is unwelcomingly patrolled by armed militia.

Fréjus is said to have been sacked by the Saracens on seven different occasions during its early history. On 2 December 1959 it also suffered what was perhaps the worst natural disaster in Provence since the 1909 earthquake. On that night the Malpasset dam on the River Reyran broke and the western districts of the town were violently flooded. 421 people were drowned and many buildings totally destroyed. Interestingly enough, and as a tribute to Roman engineering, the arena survived. A cemetery contains the bodies of those who perished and the area that was flooded is now mostly given over to market gardening and fruit production. For a while after the flood, attempts were made to grow rice.

Although hoardings on the main roads into Fréjus shout its renown as a Roman town, the medieval area around the cathedral is in many ways equally if not more rewarding. Here several buildings are constructed from sandstone, with grey-green or wine-coloured patches. (Some material may well have been pillaged from the arena.) The twelfth-century cathedral itself is curious, being doubly dedicated to Notre-Dame and Saint-Etienne. It incorporates the octagonal baptistry from an earlier, fifth-century church on this site, and is surrounded by buildings which, although ecclesiastical, are often said to be rather more military in aspect. This fascinating episcopal group is the major

one of its kind in Provence and includes the baptistry, a bishop's palace and cloisters on two floors. The cloisters are particularly interesting on account of their painted ceilings, which date from the fifteenth century and are similar to those found in the château at Tarascon. Many of the scenes depicted are quite grotesque, illustrating violent events from the Apocalypse. In an upstairs room, which is now a small archaeological museum, is the mosaic of a leopard. Presumably this was also inspired by the artist's imagination.

Covering most of the land from the coast between Toulon and Fréjus north to the motorway and the N7 is the Massif des Maures. Contrary to what some people who live in the hamlets and villages dotted across the Massif believe, its name has nothing to do with the Saracens or Moors. The origin of Maures lies in its colour – *mauram*, Latin for dark brown, and subsequently *mauro*, Provençal for black. Unlike the limestone ridges further west, the Massif des Maures is composed of various kinds of quartz, schist and granite, with the result that any light which does manage to penetrate the forest is absorbed rather than reflected. Fires have caused widespread damage here as they have to the forests further north, but even so few other parts of France are so superbly wooded, predominantly with pines, various species of oak (especially the cork oak) and chestnut trees. The oaks have been regularly cut for their timber over the last century and as a result there are increasing numbers of the *chêne pubescent*, a tree which tends to bush after harvesting. It also only loses its leaves once new growth begins, with the result that the forest as a whole is mottled by patches of brown and fawn in winter.

Approximately 60 kilometres long and 30 kilometres wide, the Massif is like an island of wooded rock. It is crossed from south to north by two roads, from Grimaud to Le Cannet and, more importantly, from Sainte-Maxime to Le Muy. Both are spectacular,

At the summit of the Col des Anges in the Massif des Maures. Track markings can be seen on the trunk of the tree.

especially the Le Cannet route which passes through the prosperous and popular village of La Garde-Freinet. Like Gassin and Ramatuelle, this was a Saracen stronghold in the tenth century. Despite its conscious attempts to appeal to tourists, the village has much charm. The old part clustered around the church has steep alleyways carved out of the rock; the newer, nineteenth-century area is much more open and grand. There are spectacular views north across the valley from the Croix des Maures, though when the wind blows towards the village from the north, the noise of the traffic from the motorway is unremitting.

La Garde-Freinet is built on the most northerly and highest of the three ridges which cross the Massif from west to east. (Geological surveys show that parts of others, now beneath the sea, account for the Iles d'Hyères and even Corsica.) Exploring this area can be a slow business, but it is immensely worthwhile. Minor roads, often in poor condition, tend to follow the valleys of streams. These drain either to the complex waterways of the Réal Martin, the Aille and the Argens, or towards the coast, or even inland into the Réal Collobrier and the Grimaud. Many of the valleys are steep-sided – rising abruptly to 400 metres – dark, wild and seemingly endless. Fire paths lead more deeply into the forests, though they are often strictly controlled and sometimes closed to the public. The highest points of the Massif are to the north of Collobrières at La Sauvette and Notre-Dame-des-Anges. Like dozens of other places throughout the hills, La Sauvette is crowned by a small chapel. Such chapels and many *oratoires* seem to be there to offer comfort to the traveller who is unsure of when he will escape from this remote and at times overpowering world. It is perhaps no accident that the *Grande Randonnée 9* avoids the interior of the Massif completely, skirting its northern edge by way of La Garde-Freinet before turning south to Port Grimaud. However well equipped and experienced, walkers

Copper-coloured trunks of harvested cork oaks.

always bring with them the potential danger of fire, and near Notre-Dame-des-Anges is a reminder – a fire-fighter's uniform draped over a frame, hanging like a grotesque crucifix.

In addition to La Garde-Freinet, Collobrières, known as the capital of the Maures, is also worth visiting. Singled out by *Le Monde* in the mid 1970s as one of the most attractive villages in the lower Var, it is now very much on the tourist map. It is most easily reached from Toulon by way of La Farlède, Solliès (where the ruined château once belonged to the Forbin family), Cuers and Pierrefeu. From Pierrefeu the road runs directly east following the Réal Collobrier between the Sommet du Peyrol to the north and Le Temple to the south. There has been a community at Collobrières since at least the eleventh century and it is said that it was here that the secrets of working with cork were first introduced into France from Spain in the Middle Ages. Cork production became a major local industry, augmented by a modest amount of

Collobrières, the centre of the *marrons glacés* industry.

159

farming. In the twentieth century, however, Collobrières has been better known for the fact that it is the centre of France's *marrons glacés* production. The village now presents some startling contrasts. The factory, with its modern equipment, smart shops and commercial slickness, is only a short walk away from houses where conditions are little better than primitive and where animals and their feed are still kept on the ground floor.

The village is overlooked from the south by the Plateau de Lambert. Some of the roads onto it are closed, but it is still possible to visit a collection of standing stones, a monument to an otherwise unrecorded civilization. For those who like walking, a way can be found across the imposing Col de Babaou and the Col de Gratteloup down into Bormes-les-Mimosas. Only a few kilometres east of Collobrières, on a rocky spur in a shallow depression surrounded by hills, is the Chartreuse de la Verne. This was a joint foundation by the bishops of Toulon and Fréjus in 1170, and was built precisely on the boundary between their parishes. In the Middle Ages it became fashionable for Provence's nobility to retire here in later life and many would elect to be buried at the monastery. Considerably damaged on a number of occasions by fire and deliberate destruction, the Chartreuse has been substantially restored and is now an historic monument. (The sale of bread baked in the original ovens makes a small contribution to its upkeep.) Like the Chartreuse of Montrieux-le-Jeune 10 kilometres north of Solliès, La Verne is idyllically peaceful. The pale pinks and reds of its roof, the yellow walls and the dark green, local serpentine rock used in splashes of decoration around doors and windows, blend beautifully with the natural surroundings.

Such pockets of beauty are not unusual in the Massif des Maures. Tiny hamlets and isolated farmhouses unexpectedly emerge from the trees. People who live here are almost always members of local families who are permanent residents – unlike so many in the Vaucluse, along the coastal strip, or on the Saint-Tropez peninsula, where there is such a high proportion of *résidences secondaires*. And although understandably wary of anyone who may be a fire hazard in the dry season, the locals have a justifiable reputation for hospitality. Their isolated world is similar to that of the Petite Crau, bypassed by people moving frantically west or east along the Provençale or clinging to the last patch of beach.

The road from Fréjus directly north to Fayence climbs gradually through pine forests, until it turns sharp right under the southern edge of the range of hills known as the Malvoisin. From this point on it becomes much more tortuous as it passes the crest of the Pic de la Gardiette. The views from here are magnificent. A whole vista of wooded hills undulating into the distance is suddenly revealed, giving some idea of the expanse and magnificence of the upper Var. Pines gradually give way to oaks and they in turn to cork oaks, whose trunks become a rich copper-orange for a while after harvesting. Deep narrow valleys become increasingly frequent as the land rises towards the Plan de Canjuers, some 20 kilometres further north. Dry in summer, they are nearly all busy with fast-moving streams in winter and spring. And after rain, especially in the autumn, the interior of the dense surrounding forest gives off a smell of damp, rotting vegetation that is quite free from any human pollution. The atmosphere and water in these hills is so pure that many of the villages are now sought after by the retired or have become small centres for convalescence.

The road from Fréjus to Fayence (D4) gives many opportunities for exploring the interior. To the west are the Gorges de Malvoisin or, slightly further and most easily reached from the main road to Draguignan, the splendid waterfall at Pennafort; to the east the various tributaries of the Reyran lose themselves in the Bois de l'Ermite. The first village after leaving Fréjus is Bagnols-en-Forêt, which lies just off the main road. From the south the entrance is straightforward, but from the main road to the northwest it is necessary to turn back into the village round a tight hairpin bend.

Bormes-les-Mimosas: a riot of yellow in the early summer.

Left Seclusion: the Chartreuse de la Verne.   *Above* The valley below the waterfall at Pennafort.

This leads into the narrow main street running between houses clamped to the hillside like the steps in an amphitheatre. A village has been here for hundreds of years, but Bagnols is now being rapidly modernized. Some people find the slow commuter journey into Fréjus worth the effort, and in recent years a small expensive residential development has appeared. As its name suggests, the village overlooks a huge clearing encircled by forest. Directly west is the steep escarpment of the Bois du Rouet, capped by some rocks whose ruin-like formations have led to the name of Castel Diao, or Devil's Castle. There are also outcrops of porphyry here, the purple colour of the rock contrasting sharply with the browns and greens of the forest.

Five kilometres further north the road drops down into Saint-Paul-en-Forêt, a quiet village which was renowned for glass-making in the seventeenth century. Local tradition claims – though without much evidence – that Louis XII's wife Jeanne once passed through the village and that the huge glass jars – *bonbonnes* (demijohns in English) – were known as Dames Jeannes from that time. Saint-Paul is one of those villages which seems to belong to the past and is all too easily ignored. A splendid squat, solid building with large turrets, referred to locally as the Château de Queylard, stands in the centre of the village. This is certainly a token of Saint-Paul's past stature, as is the equally misnamed Château Grime just to the east. Like Bagnols, Saint-Paul today is very much a dormitory village for Fréjus or Fayence, though it has an active broom- and pipe-making industry of its own. These and other local products can be bought at a very lively fair held in late January. It is also an admirable departure point for excursions by road and forest paths, either east in the direction of the lake of Saint Cassien or west into the 'Royal Forest' and the attractive valley of the Méaulx.

The road directly north crosses yet another massive

Fayence, beyond which lies some of the most spectacular countryside of the upper Var.

open space (round the D562) where room has been found for a small airfield. But it is more rewarding to approach Fayence from the southeast, past the large, well-maintained Château Bouge and thence by way of Tourrettes. Here there is a most curious house, a copy of a Russian military building designed in the early nineteenth century by one Colonel Fabre, who had worked as an engineer for Tsar Nicholas I. From both Tourrettes and Fayence, less than a kilometre away, the views northwest are reminders that these villages are in the first foothills of the southern Alps. Their climate, like their situation, is most agreeable. The name Fayence in fact derives from *faventia loca* or favourable place – and the population has more than trebled since the 1920s. Farming and traditional artisanal crafts in pottery, leather (especially saddles) and woodwork continue to flourish, and some light industry (and the airfield) has developed since World War 2. Now being vigorously restored, old Fayence is yet another example of a medieval fortified village, and the Pharmacie Tallent is noted for its wood-carving and its fine collection of *faïence* pots.

Beyond Fayence the road soon penetrates some of the Var's most spectacular areas. Within less than 10 kilometres it reaches the steep southern edge of the Plan de Canjuers, a wild expanse of more than 40,000 hectares, as high as the Massif Central and with as much snow in winter. This has always been one of the most desolate parts of France, with a severe climate for much of the year, no valleys to provide shelter and few settlements. Even the grass is poor and the few hardy sheep that graze it are brought down in the winter. Even in summer Brovès, the largest community, had fewer than a hundred inhabitants, while further west Vérignon, just at the edge of the plateau, still has no more than about two dozen. In the late 1960s the government decided that the whole area – like the Plateau d'Albion – should be handed over to the military. Inevitably there was token resistance, and some people in villages just to the south have remained uneasy about what is going on; others dismiss it with a wave of the hand and a shrug of the shoulders. The *avens*, like those at Albion though fewer in number, have been developed as experimental units and the whole area exudes mystery and secrecy. It can be reached and crossed either from the junction of roads known as La Magdeleine west of Fayence or, more spectacularly, by way of the Col du Bel Homme at over 1000 metres.

The group of villages between Fayence and La Magdeleine were once fortified and clearly virtually impregnable. Seillans is the first, oval in shape and overlooking the plain surrounding Fayence. Much of the medieval wall remains, as does a splendid gate known as the Porte Sarrasine and sections of an underground passage which once ringed the village. In the centre are some especially fine sixteenth-century houses and carvings of signs denoting different trades can be seen on a number of key-stones in arches above doors and windows. Less than 15 kilometres further west is Bargemon, an equally self-contained village, so shaded by plane trees that even in summer it can seem like a pool of darkness. It too recalls its past; four twelfth-century gates remain, as do parts of the defensive walls. Both villages contain convalescent and retirement homes and Bargemon in particular is noted for the purity of its water and its gentle climate.

Yet these can be wild parts. In the depths of winter snow can make the roads impassable and storms seem to bounce off the face of the hills immediately to the north. At night too the sense of isolation in either of these villages – as in those of the Lubéron for example – can be acute. And it is even more so in the smaller communities of Callas and Claviers just to the south. Each is delightfully pretty and still characteristically medieval in design. Guidebooks from the 1920s record these villages as being 'almost inaccessible', and road communication today, while adequate, is hardly lavish. It is possible to walk from Seillans to Claviers along the crest of the ridge known as La Pigne, but although very dramatic, the terrain is not easy. Arguably the best way to explore this whole heavily wooded and hilly pocket of the Var is by local bus. The French who pound up the hills on their lightweight bicycles and hurtle down into the valleys seem to do so with their eyes closed.

Draguignan to the southwest of Bargemon is said to owe its name to *drak*, a Celtic word for dragon. Like the *tarasque* or the *couloubre*, this beast also met its match in a Christian hero – St Hermentaire. Another strange relic from the past is the Pierre de la Fée – or Peïro de la Fado in Provençal – just to the northwest of the town, a huge dolmen supported by three standing stones. It is 'protected' by three trees, an oak, a juniper and a lotus – all three sacred in Celtic mythology. This site and other remains testify to the fact that primitive people lived here long before the Romans came. Despite being decimated by the plague, the town became an important commercial centre in the Middle Ages – a fact still reflected in many of the street names. Its subsequent history was turbulent, with the Wars of Religion causing extensive damage. By the nineteenth century, however, Draguignan's prosperity had revived and it has continued to thrive ever since. It is an important centre for tourism (in spite of an above-average rainfall) and, like Apt, it has benefited from the proximity of a large-scale military establishment.

Set on a small chalk plateau, Draguignan is a most attractive town. Its clock tower is one of the finest in Provence and other outstanding features include the carved lintels on some handsome medieval houses, the so-called Maison de la Reine Jeanne in the rue de Trans, with its superb Renaissance interior, and the early nineteenth-century façade to the theatre. The museum displays paintings by Boucher, Mignard and Rembrandt and there is also a fine collection of *faïence* from Moustiers and Marseille.

An alternative route to Draguignan from Bargemon by way of the Gorges de Châteaudouble is a particularly attractive one. Only 2 kilometres or so out of Bargemon are the remains of two villages. There is not much worth seeing at Baudrom, but the primitive chapel at Favas has been beautifully restored. Built of local stone, it is set just to the north of the road in a shallow depression. Thereafter the road rises towards

Only fifty years ago villages like Callas were virtually unreachable.

The huge dolmen known as Pierre de la Fée,
Draguignan.

the main southern entrance to the Camp de Canjuers before doubling sharply back to Montferrat (another village undergoing development) and entering the Gorges de Châteaudouble. Although on a smaller scale and less spectacular than those of La Nesque (see p. 34–6), these gorges should not be missed. The views from Rebouillon to the south (an ancient fortified village built on a narrow spur of rock), or from Châteaudouble itself to the north, are particularly impressive. Rebouillon has the added attraction of being close to one of the most interesting and well-known grottos in the region, the Grotte des Chauves-souris. The rock formations here are some of the finest in Provence and there are important skeletons of prehistoric animals, including lions. Perhaps the mosaic of the leopard in Fréjus is not so fanciful after all.

Slightly to the west of Châteaudouble is Ampus, situated in a fertile plain surrounded by woods. A dramatic ridge of white limestone running south from here joins the gorges half-way between Châteaudouble and Rebouillon. The village itself sits above the road at the end of this ridge, on the route of the Via Aurelia as it came up from Fréjus. It was here too that the Saracens were defeated, a victory celebrated by the building of the chapel of Notre-Dame-de-Spéluque. This is perhaps the most interesting building in Ampus and contains a magnificent and unusual altar, the main table of which is supported by three plain and two twisted columns. Ampus has recently been developed as a holiday centre, especially for parties of school children, and as a result the village is more prosperous than it has been for many years.

From Ampus the road threads its way across a sandy landscape and through pine forests towards Tourtour. About 3 kilometres before the village there is an unexpected modern residential development (Saint-Pierre-de-Tourtour), which is highly fashionable during summer months. The climate of this area is extremely agreeable and Tourtour is important all the year round as a convalescent centre. Known as the 'village in the sky', its natural site and advantages have been fully and tastefully developed and it is arguably the prettiest village in this part of the Var. Many of its houses are built in pale, locally quarried stone and the village is threaded by neatly channelled streams which provide a constant and restful background accompaniment to daily life. The main square is lined by restaurants and is the site of frequent markets. Two enormous elm trees here (the *ormeaux* de Sully) were planted in 1639 to commemorate a visit by Anne of Austria. Other features include parts of the twelfth-century fortifications and gateways, the sixteenth-century château (restored) and a seventeenth-century oil-mill, all reminders of Tourtour's prosperity in different periods.

Delightfully attractive itself, Tourtour is also an

The wrought iron on this former clock tower in Draguignan is some of the best in Provence.

Above **The unspoiled medieval village of Entrecasteaux, east of Cotignac.**

Right Publicité varoise **in Brignoles.**

ideal centre for excursions into the surrounding area. Aups to the northwest is reached by a road running along the edge of the limestone ridge known as Des Espiguières, which rises to nearly 1000 metres. This is an area that has suffered from fires and is no longer as thickly wooded as it once was. Two houses in the shallow valley to the south of the road have escaped damage, however, and should not be missed. The first, La Beaume, has an unusually well-preserved Provençal pigeon-loft; the second, Taurenne, is a striking sixteenth-century fortified farmhouse containing some fine tapestries and an excellent collection of Provençal furniture.

Aups is the most important administrative community in the upper Var after Draguignan. The old village, built into the side of the hill, now stands to the east of the main centre. Developed between the seventeenth and nineteenth centuries, the domestic buildings from this period in Aups form one of the best groups of their kind in Provence. The village is also famous for its seven sundials, all individually named. At least one of them is the work of an abbé Jean, an eighteenth-century scholar who also devised a map (based on strict mathematical calculations) which proved Aups to be the centre of the world. This can be seen in La Fabrique, the house in which the abbé Jean lived and which is now appropriately owned by the local Syndicat d'Initiative. Whatever the significance of the abbé's work, Aups is unquestionably a gastronomic centre. Local lamb marinated and roasted with thyme, or thrushes with juniper berries, are much appreciated by local people and tourists alike. During the summer Aups becomes a lively craft centre and attracts a good number of colourful and largely young visitors; but during the winter it is a rather sedate, almost pompous place. Somehow the spirit of the abbé Jean lives on.

To the southwest of Tourtour lie a number of

Les Grands Escaliers. Part of the labyrinth of vaulted streets and passages in the old town at Brignoles.

villages quite different in character from Aups yet unique in their own right. The first, Villecroze, is still partly ruined, yet is fast becoming fashionable. Like Salernes and Cotignac only a few kilometres further on, it owes much of its attractiveness to the great wall of rock (over 500 metres high) which dominates it. This is an extension of the Espiguières ridge between Tourtour and Aups, which here bends round from the northeast in a natural protective arc. The whole ridge is riddled with grottos, many of which, as in other parts of Provence, have been found to contain evidence of prehistoric settlement. One on the north side of the village is particularly extraordinary. In the sixteenth century a local nobleman transformed it into a four-storeyed house of substance, and remains of the staircases and mullions which he cut out of the natural rock can still be seen.

From Villecroze the most attractive route follows the cliff crossing the southern tip of the Gorge de Plérimond, a fault in the fertile area known as the Huchanne which lies to the south of Aups. Salernes, the next village, is centred on the River Bresque, once a source of power for several local industries, including pottery, tiles, silk and weaving. Unlike, say, Fayence, Salernes is still the same size as it was earlier in the century, though it is the centre for the production of the famous hexagonal Provençal floor-tiles known as *tomettes*, which are made from local red clay. Squeezed between the hills, Salernes is not unattractive and enjoys an agreeable climate for most of the year. But, as at Cotignac, there is no impression of a thriving community, and perhaps both these places are overshadowed by Draguignan and Aups.

As well as the many grottos in the area, there are also a number of waterfalls and underground lakes. One of the most spectacular waterfalls is just outside the tiny walled village of Sillans, half-way between Salernes and Cotignac. The main fall (42 metres) cascades into a complex of deep, green pools, where local fishermen catch excellent trout, some of which soon find their way to local restaurants. There is a well-worn path to it from the main road, but it is worth clambering around some of the smaller pools to explore this whole

Above Symbols of wisdom and authority on the doors of the fifteenth-century palace of the comtes de Provence in Brignoles.

Right Chapel of Notre-Dame-du-Carami near Carcès.

Church window, Carcès.

---

delightfully wooded area and those who like walking could make their way back to Salernes or on to Cotignac.

Of this group of villages within easy distance of Tourtour, Cotignac is the biggest, being about the same size as Aups. Like Salernes, it was once more thriving than it appears to be now and it has not grown in size since the beginning of the century. Its one-time prosperity is recorded in some elegant seventeenth-century architecture, and the rue de Jérusalem and the quartier de la Synagogue indicate that there was once a substantial Jewish community here. In recent years there have been indications that the village is becoming aware of its tourist potential. Its main attraction lies, once again, in natural formations. Cotignac sits literally at the very bottom of a sheer cliff, 80 metres high and 400 metres long. The rock is pierced high up by a series of superb grottos and over 200 metres of corridors, culminating in the aptly

named Salle des Merveilles (Hall of Marvels). The stone of these caves is brilliant white and the stalactite formations are some of the best in the south of France, including those to be found in the Ardèche. At present these wonders can only be reached by an extremely precarious route. A path at the foot of the cliff (passing some 'modernized' and inhabited caves) leads to an ascent involving a series of rusted iron spiral staircases, crude concrete ledges and narrow passages shorn up by wood. The rewards for those who reach the top are spectacular, but they are gained only with the expenditure of considerable effort and nervous tension. This is not a climb for the faint-hearted!

From Cotignac it is an easy journey south to Brignoles and the motorway, or west via Barjols and thence to Saint-Maximin or Aix. Modern society rapidly reappears once out of the forests and hills and into the valley. A more interesting route across this southern edge of the upper Var is to take the road to Carcès and then turn east to Le Thoronet, joining the main valley to the south at Le Luc.

Just south of Carcès is an artificial lake, created in 1936 and the source of Toulon's domestic water. A good walk from its eastern edge leads along a wooded ridge and down into the forest of La Darboussière, where the abbey of Le Thoronet is sited. Founded in the mid twelfth century, Thoronet is older than both Silvacane and Sénanque, and is undoubtedly the most attractive of the 'three sisters of Provence'. Built in the remarkably short period of forty years, it has a unity of style that is not matched by any other group of religious buildings elsewhere in Provence.

In true Cistercian tradition the abbey sits in a depression as a sign of humility, but this valley is not the wild gorge of Sénanque. The contours here are gentle and the pale reddish stone from which much of Thoronet is built is beautifully offset by the

---

The abbey of Le Thoronet. The farm gates are a reminder that this was once a working community and not just a place for meditation.

background of trees. A further indication of Cistercian humility is the almost total absence of decoration. Only on the capitals in the chapter house is the severe austerity of this order modified by some modest scrolls and carvings of flowers. Superbly restored, Thoronet offers a prime illustration of a monastic community in all its religious and domestic aspects. On dull, overcast days it requires little effort to imagine how harsh life must have been on occasions. Walking in the gardens with their cypress trees on a summer's evening, when the cloisters are still warm from the heat of the day, and when the strains of a string quartet or a Gregorian chant drift from the nave of the main church, peace can seem absolute.

From Thoronet, paths and roads lead southwest to the end of a narrow ridge, the Montagne des Ubacs, which descends abruptly to the attractive village of Le Vieux-Cannet, 7 or 8 kilometres further south. From here, the mid-point between Toulon and Fréjus, there are especially fine views (over the motorway 300 metres below) across the Maures towards La Garde-Freinet on the road to Grimaud and Saint-Tropez. And only 4 kilometres away to the east is Le Luc, a town of some administrative importance in this part of Provence and whose population has more than doubled since the 1950s, a fact reflected in a number of rather unattractive high-rise buildings. Prosperous under the Romans because of its position on the Via Aurelia, Le Luc had previously been the site of a number of different Celtic camps. Later, in the sixteenth century, it was selected as one of the towns in Provence where the Protestants could practise their beliefs without interference, and the presence of this religious community ensured prosperity in the same way that Jewish communities did elsewhere.

Today the nearby aerodrome just to the east of Le Cannet-des-Maures guarantees a regular source of income, and Le Luc also benefits from the presence of the administration responsible for much of Provence's

Enjoying the autumn sun in Cabasse.

water supply. Unfortunately the historic fabric of the town is being eroded by such modern developments and by the amount of through traffic. Although the church with its hexagonal bell tower is now a listed building, it is in dire need of proper restoration.

But like so many other places in Provence which have gradually yielded to the encroachment and demands of the twentieth century, some traditions and superstitions from the past stubbornly persist. Le Luc derives its name from *lucus*, a magic wood, and at night even the presence of the autoroute cannot dispel a sense of eeriness, especially in the hills just to the west of the town. More practically, local folklore has it that a sure cure for whooping cough is to pass children seven times from left to right under the stomach of a donkey!

The fountain at Cabasse, south of Le Thoronet.

179

Buech

Sisteron

Jabron

Valbelle ●

*Montagne de
Lure*

Salignac ●

Volonne ●

Château-Arnoux ●
Mallefougasse

Les Sieyes ● ● Digne

Cruis ●

Malijai ●

● Les Dourbes

Lardiers ●

St-Etienne ●

Les Mées ● Espinouse

Banon ●

Ongles ●

Bléone

● Entrages

Sigonce ●

Puimichel ●

St-André-les-Alpes ●

Entrevaux ●

Forcalquier ●
Mane ●

Lurs ●

Entrevennes ●

Bras-d'Asse ●

St-Maime ●
Dauphin ●

Oraison ●

Asse

Puimoisson ●

Blieux ●

Colostre

Apt ●

● Moustiers-
Ste-Marie

Castellane ●

*Montagne
du
Lubéron*

Manosque ●

Valensole ●

Riez ●

Pierrevert ●

Rougon ●

Grambois ●

St-Martin-
de-Brômes ●

Allemagne-
en-Provence ●

La Palud-
sur-Verdon ●

Trigance ●

Gréoux-les-Bains ●

● Les-Salles-
sur-Verdon

Jabron

La Tour-d'Aigues ●

Vinon-sur-Verdon ●

Esparron-
de-Verdon ●

Pertuis ●
Mirabeau ●

St-Julien ●

Verdon

● Quinson

Grasse ●

Durance

Jouques ●

Rians ●

5
The Heartland of Provence

Sisteron – Montagne de Lure – Forcalquier –
Manosque – Gréoux – Riez – Moustiers – Gorges
du Verdon – Castellane – Valensole – Digne

On 5 August 1942 the bodies of the British biochemist and dietician Sir Jack Drummond, his wife and daughter were discovered just outside the village of Lurs, not far from the main road running alongside the Durance. The parents had been shot, the daughter clubbed to death. There was no apparent motive for the killings. The incident was reported by a local peasant farmer Gustave Dominici who, later confessing that the child had still been breathing when he had first found her, was given a two-month prison sentence for not summoning assistance. Beyond that, and despite extensive police enquiries, no conclusions were reached. Two years later Gustave's father Gaston Dominici was arrested. At first he confessed to the crime but later retracted, claiming that the police had drugged his coffee in order to force him to admit guilt. The second son Clovis maintained his father was guilty, but Gustave who initially agreed with him then changed his mind. At the same time he alleged there were other factors involved, but that he would not talk about them. Court scenes were frequently rowdy as father and sons hurled abuse at one another. Gaston Dominici was finally found guilty and condemned to death. The Director of Public Prosecutions ordered the trial to be re-opened, however, and although the first verdict was upheld, the death penalty was waived. Gaston Dominici was then 78.

At the time the case was widely reported throughout Europe. The popular French press in particular carried countless stories and speculations about family feuds and about the enclosed, secretive nature of this peasant world. Reference was frequently made to *omertá*, a Sicilian word meaning refusal to bear witness against a relative or neighbour. Pictures showed a series of proud, defiant, hostile men whose eyes gave nothing away.

For such a crime to remain unsolved in the middle of the twentieth century, even in a relatively remote area of France, seems barely credible. Yet many of the qualities which it reveals are echoed in the works of Jean Giono (1895–1970), the greatest of modern Provençal novelists, who came from Manosque only 20 kilometres away. In novels such as *Le Chant du monde*, *Un de Baumugnes* or *Le Grand Troupeau* Giono depicts a world in which the forces of nature are supreme. The happiness generated by spring is balanced by the dark and mysterious forces of winter. The system of rewards and punishments is primitive and quite separate from any imposed or devised by 'civilized' society. Intuition is all. Clara, a blind girl in *Le Chant du monde*, has, as her name suggests, a greater perception of the world about her than many who can see. When Ragotaz in *Le Grand Troupeau* is killed, his blood soaks into the soil like the resin of the trees he has loved all

his life and which have now been savagely destroyed by war. Families are tribal, emotions are basic, values absolute and uncompromising.

Such an atmosphere still prevails in many parts of this region, which some regard as the only remaining authentic part of Provence. Although this may not be entirely true, there is little or nothing here of the brashness and superficiality to be found in many of the popular tourist centres, especially on the coast. For those who want to glean some impression of the harsher and more mysterious aspects of Provençal life, this northeast segment is as good a place to begin as any.

It is entered through the Porte de Provence at Sisteron, where the massive wall of rock rising 500 metres above the town appears to have been cleft by the Durance in its rush south from the Dauphiné. Today the two main roads and the railway squeeze through a valley no more than a few hundred metres wide, and the plan to bring a motorway here in the year 2000 will require yet another feat of imaginative and massive engineering. Yet Sisteron's prosperity depends very much on its being in the forefront of such modern developments. A huge underground hydro-electric complex near the industrial area 10 kilometres to the north is a vital link in the chain of stations which follows the river down to Mallemort in the Bouches-du-Rhône. Tourism too is important. There are good routes to the Alps and beyond to Switzerland; while in the opposite direction the Riviera is easily reached by way of Castellane and Grasse or through the Var valley to Nice; even without the motorway Aix and Marseille are only two hours away. And the care given to the preservation of buildings and the network of well-indicated walks through the old streets is testimony to the awareness of how valuable a transient population is during much of the year.

Sisteron has experienced more upheaval and disruption than most Provençal towns. Originally the

---

Light and shade in Lurs.

disputed site of Ligurian settlements, it was captured by the Romans in 25 BC and developed by them into an important centre, only to be ravaged by the Saracens. It was decimated by the plague in the fifteenth century, torn by the Wars of Religion and finally badly bombed by American planes on 15 August 1944. Yet there is little to show for these disasters now and local people are justly proud of the restoration work that has been accomplished. With its labyrinth of vaulted streets (andrônes), tiny squares and unexpected stairways, this is a town to be explored on foot, with a visit to the citadel as the culmination of the tour. This austere fortress dominating the entire town was begun in the fourteenth century on the site of an earlier château and was substantially modified during the next two hundred years. Virtually impregnable, it has served as a prison for people of all nationalities and rank, including the future king of Poland in the seventeenth century, and political prisoners during the German Occupation. With its immaculately tended lawns and austere grey stone, both the scale and site of the building are impressive. It is built to follow the contours of the rock and to the north and east offers vertiginous views over the Dauphiné and the Durance hundreds of metres below.

There is a strong sense of being poised between two regions and two cultures here, an impression reinforced in the town itself by the twelfth-century cathedral of Notre-Dame. This large, well-proportioned building is in many respects typically romanesque, but its octagonal tower and rather delicate external gallery are far more reminiscent of Alpine or northern Italian architecture than Provençal. For those who can, Sisteron should be visited in the autumn, when the customary blues are darkened by a thin veil of mist to give the distinctive light known locally as *l'heure mauve*.

From Sisteron the Durance flows almost directly south past Château-Arnoux, Oraison and Manosque until it sweeps round to join the Rhône south of the Lubéron hills. To the west are two parallel ranges of mountains, the northern one marking the edge of Provence and eventually joining the Baronnies to the

Above **Houses stacked against one another at Sisteron.**

Right **The northeastern gateway to Provence: one of the most extraordinary rock formations in the south of France.**

north of the Ventoux. These ranges are divided by the Jabron river, which flows into the Durance about 5 kilometres south of Sisteron and is itself fed by dozens of streams known here as *torrents*, fierce when swollen by melted snow and indicative of the local terrain. To the south of the Jabron is the range of the Montagne de Lure, just over 30 kilometres long and rising to nearly 2000 metres. Like the Mont Ventoux, the Lure offers only one road across its summit. This winds up from the Jabron valley through the tiny community of Valbelle and then zigzags to the Pas de la Graille and the summit before descending to Saint-Etienne some 14 kilometres away on the southern side.

It is equally possible – and more rewarding – to follow the *Grande Randonnée 6* from Sisteron. This is a long, hard walk, but those who embark on it can take advantage of an adequately equipped if basic hut just after the summit. At Valbelle it is worth making a detour to the Chapelle de Saint-Pons and the Trou de Saint-Pons, a small tube-like cave. The path to the cave is precipitous and crosses a seemingly precarious bridge which requires agility of foot as much as strength of nerve. The path from Valbelle leads, as the village's name ('beautiful valley') suggests, to some splendid scenery, nowhere more so perhaps than when it passes between two outcrops of rock, the Montagnes de Pélegrine and de Sumiou. For much of the way it doubles the old *piste des jas*, the ancient track linking isolated farmsteads, and with care can be left in order to follow forest and fire paths back north to the Jabron or down the more extensive and wooded valleys stretching towards Banon, Ongles, Saint-Etienne, Cruis, or the attractive hamlet of Mallefougasse.

With the possible exception of some of the more remote parts of the Massif de la Sainte Baume, the Lure is the least well known and least frequented of the Provençal mountain ranges. To some extent this is understandable. The climate is marginally less reliable than in some areas further south and the whole region

Saint-Etienne, tucked in gracefully against the southern slopes of the Lure mountains.

belongs more naturally to the mountains to the north in the department of Hautes-Alpes. There is also a bleakness about much of the southwestern part of the range where it joins the Plateau d'Albion. Two hundred years ago many of these villages on the southern edge of the Lure each had several hundred people in them; today populations frequently number less than a hundred.

Yet the natural richness and attractiveness of the region should not be underestimated. Magnificent trees (beech, pines and oaks), abundant flora (some of it rare), herbs and animal life (from foxes to wild goats), together with the generally chaotic terrain combine to make this an endlessly exciting region to explore. And even half-deserted villages contain unexpected delights – arcaded streets in Banon (and the local goat's cheese), grottos with stalactites near Lardiers northeast of Banon, wild asparagus and the ruins of a village estimated to be a thousand years old at Ongles, and the local herby liqueur at Saint-Etienne. The attractions of Cruis include the remains of some gothic cloisters and, just north of the village, the *abîme* (abyss) into which, according to local tradition, women guilty of adultery were once cast. The lower southern slopes of the mountains are dotted with dry-stone sheep-pens and primitive farmhouses, sometimes built with material brought through the woods from the bed of the Durance. Life in this part of Provence was hard, and in many respects still is.

Between the southern edge of the Lure and the hills overlooking the east bank of the Durance lies the Commune de Montlaux, centred on the principal village of Sigonce. Here, as further south around Forcalquier, the soil is poor and the water supply barely adequate, even with modern methods of irrigation. Almonds, olives and the vine are cultivated – the local wine, the Coteaux de Pierrevert, can be surprisingly good – and there is some sheep-farming. Various paths lead from Montlaux into the Bois d'Aris northwest of Lurs and onto a small tree-covered plateau 700 metres above the river. Here, not far from the Durance, is the priory of Ganagobie. Set amongst junipers, oaks and pines, it dates from the twelfth century and is built on a site originally occupied by three churches at least two hundred years older. Some of the buildings are in good repair, notably the cloisters and the main church. The latter has a triple-arched entrance with a pronounced design involving quite large lobe-like carvings thought by some to be eastern in origin. There is also a Roman mosaic, on which an elephant, a lion, a griffon and other mythological monsters fighting with horsemen are depicted. These animals recall the leopard in Fréjus and may well also have been inspired by creatures seen in the east. A more recent addition is a somewhat indifferent picture of the Virgin Mary in the main nave, by the nineteenth-century painter Adolphe Monticelli, who is seen to better advantage in the museum of his native Marseille. Monticelli's work is characterized by thickly-applied paint and strong brush strokes and was one of the principal reasons why Van Gogh was attracted to Provence. When and by whom this particular painting was commissioned remains unclear.

Ganagobie is worth visiting for all these reasons, but especially for its views over the Durance and north towards the Lure mountains. From the western edge of this 'island in the sky', a road twists down through the woods, over a second-century bridge and into the village of Lurs.

Just southwest of Sigonce is the bustling community of Forcalquier, aroused from its rural torpor in recent years with the growth of artisanal activities, the search for *résidences secondaires* and an attempt to promote local food and wine. (The promised motorway is also influential, of course, and its eventual arrival could bring economic benefit to the whole region.) Time was, however, when Forcalquier enjoyed considerable religious, administrative and cultural importance. Until Henri IV destroyed its château in 1601, it was the capital of Haute-Provence and had achieved independent status. Much in the town bears witness to that importance and prosperity: fine town houses with elegantly worked doors and windows; the whole Jewish quarter around its synagogue (less impressive than the one at Carpentras perhaps but just as

significant); the streets in the carefully restored *quartiers* of Saint Pancrace and Bonbardière, or the Couvent des Cordeliers now used for exhibitions and concerts.

The view from the chapel of Notre-Dame-de-Provence on top of a hill to the southeast shows clearly how the village developed around the curve of the hills. Notre-Dame is interesting too in its own right, in that its rather unusual Byzantine decor and style recall Notre-Dame-de-la-Garde (see p. 64) and the cathedral in Marseille. The chapel is adjoined by what is possibly the best-kept cemetery in the whole of Provence, much admired for its neatly clipped and shaped yew trees and small, round, pointed, stone huts. These are known locally as *cabanons* and are to be found over quite a wide area around Forcalquier. Like the *bories* near Gordes, many were inhabited up to the turn of the century.

Forcalquier is an ideal centre from which to explore all this area of the Alpes-de-Haute-Provence to the west of the Durance. Just to the north of the town are Les Mourres, rocks weathered into the shape of human heads and said to be the spirits of Moors who laid siege to the town in the eleventh century (but who eventually established friendly relations with the local inhabitants). To the south is the village of Mane clustered around its fortress. This is a well-preserved place whose attractions include the citadel with its turrets, sixteenth- and seventeenth-century houses built from local stone, the plaster-moulded chimney-piece in the Hôtel de Miravail and Notre-Dame-de-Salagon, a superb example of a twelfth-century romanesque church. But the crowning feature of the town is the Château de Sauvan just to the south on the road to Apt. For long known as 'Le Petit Trianon Provençal' and worth comparing with the more compact Château de la Gaude near Aix, this magnificent building is a real oasis of classical beauty. Designed early in the eighteenth century by J-B

The old citadel overlooking the town of Forcalquier.

Franque, it was finished within the amazingly short time of twenty years, despite the interruption of an outbreak of plague. The proportions of windows, balconies, columns and magnificent entrance porch blend perfectly, and the whole building has weathered over the centuries into the colour of pale honey. The interior is as grand and as well composed as the exterior. From an entrance hall with four imposing columns, a stone staircase with wrought-iron balustrade winds up to the first floor, where the principal reception room is no less than 84 metres long. Only the grounds at Sauvan could possibly disappoint. Despite the south-facing terrace and the statutory ornamental pond reflecting the eastern façade, the *parc* seems unplanned. But with views to the Lure in the north and the Lubéron only a few kilometres to the south, the splendid situation is compensation enough.

From Sauvan a minor road runs south across a small, bleak plain passing close to the villages of Saint-Maîme, where lignite is mined, and Dauphin, a good example of a *village perché*. Just to the west across some low wooded hills is the Observatoire de Haute Provence. In 1957, flying saucers are said to have been sighted here. A kilometre or so after Dauphin the road begins to climb and enters the national park of the Lubéron. At nearly 600 metres it crosses the Col de la Mort d'Imbert, skirts the peak of the Mont des Espels and drops down to Manosque.

Like Avignon or Arles, Manosque has suffered from the unplanned development of light industry, and some of the immediate surrounding area is scarred by mining. To the east the alluvial plain of the Durance is criss-crossed by artificial waterways, railway lines and wind-breaks, and dotted with innumerable smallholdings. But the old town, packed in tightly behind its walls, has retained all its Provençal charm, despite a population that has increased fourfold since just after World War 1 and is still growing.

Angelic flute player on the citadel at Forcalquier, with audience and romanesque arches.

Originally the site of a Ligurian settlement (*manoc* means many springs; *asq*, river), Manosque enjoys what is generally considered to be one of the best climates in the whole of France. Like most strategically placed towns, it has had a turbulent history. It was fortified during the Middle Ages, but only two of the original five gates have survived – the Porte Saunerie to the south and the Porte Soubeyran, restored in the nineteenth century, to the north. The latter sports a rather fine, onion-shaped belfry. Elsewhere lumps of the medieval walls can still be seen in the façades of modern buildings. Much of the walled town is now pedestrianized and as this area is only a square kilometre in extent, it is easily explored. Even on Saturday, the principal market day, there is an abrupt change from the noisy boulevards which follow the line of the old walls to the inner town.

There are no particularly exceptional buildings here, but the eighteenth-century town hall is notable. So too is the church of Saint-Sauveur, partly because of its romanesque arches but more particularly for its statue of the Black Virgin. This is known as Notre Dame du Romigier, since it is said to have been found in a thorn bush (*romigier* is *roncier* in modern French). Legend also claims that the monks who built the church found the statue so ugly that on several occasions they left it outside; it would repeatedly return to the high altar of its own accord. . . . Some people today still believe that the Virgin has power to bring rain during periods of drought. Miraculous qualities apart, what is striking about both Virgin and Child is that they look almost oriental and have the tranquillity associated with Buddhist statues. Beneath all these buildings there runs an almost complete labyrinth of interconnecting cellars and passages. Those lucky enough to be invited to visit them will be taken literally into an underworld. Despite the fact modern produce is often stored here, these subterranean passages recall the secretive and closed world so typical of many Provençal villages even less than a century ago.

By contrast, the open, expanding environs of Manosque and a busy bus station are emblems of a new

191

Left **Manosque: place de l'Hôtel de Ville.**

Above **Bloche's statue *Le Froid* in Manosque – a reminder of the harsh side of Provençal weather.**

193

Former ice house near Mirabeau.

world. The atomic station at Cadarache on the Durance to the south has been a principal reason for the growth of population and has made a major contribution to the town's prosperity. But people living here also commute to Aix, less than 60 kilometres away, and even to Marseille. Manosque has succeeded in retaining a nice balance between what is still in many respects a strong Provençal agricultural community and a modern technocratic one.

Those who do commute follow the main road along the valley of the Durance to Meyrargues before dipping south, a route that is more attractive than many main roads in this part of France. A more leisurely and rewarding way is to leave Manosque to

the southwest, skirting the Mont Toutes Aures through Pierrevert (an important local wine centre where a splendid *fête des vins* is held in mid August every year), and making for Grambois at the edge of the southern slopes of the Lubéron. Set in the wooded valley of the Lèze on a sharp escarpment, Grambois is an excellent example of a *village perché* built up on various levels and containing an amazing number of pigeon-lofts. A picturesque road (running parallel to the *Grande Randonnée 9*) cuts across the hills southeast to Mirabeau. The turreted château (owned in the late nineteenth century by the right-wing politician and writer Maurice Barrès) has a magnificent view over the valley of the Durance.

Turning back to the west, it is worth making a slight detour north in order to visit La Tour-d'Aigues, where the remains of the sixteenth-century château include a triumphal arch which bears a striking resemblance to the one at Orange. Thereafter, once more following the valley of the Lèze, the road drops down to Pertuis.

Despite an influx of people working in the local hydro-electric stations or at Cadarache, just 20 kilometres to the east, Pertuis has succeeded in retaining much of its charm. The land around is intensively cultivated, many of the smallholdings amounting to no more than 10 hectares. Potatoes, tomatoes and wheat are the principal products, though the danger of a late spring frost caused by the currents of cold air rushing down the river valley means young crops have to be protected by hundreds of strips of plastic. Although now more than 2 kilometres from the river, Pertuis once controlled an important shipping toll and was the capital of the lower Durance. There is local evidence of very ancient settlements and in the Middle Ages it was linked with the religious communities at Montmajour and Forcalquier. Only a clock tower now remains of the thirteenth-century château, but there are some fine classical houses from the seventeenth and eighteenth centuries, built by the stone masons who worked in and around Aix. The ornate Italianate front of the Maison de la Reine Jeanne, the second wife of King René, is also noteworthy.

From Pertuis it is best to cross the river and then branch immediately east past the isolated and somewhat grandiosely named Château de Repentance to Peyrolles. Here the road forks. To the east it runs between hills to Jouques and thence to Rians. To the north it follows the Durance up to the Pont Mirabeau and on to Vinon-sur-Verdon. A wooded area (principally oaks and pines) lies between the two, the northern part of which is occupied by the nuclear research station with its domes, chimneys, radio masts and fences. This is understandably closed to the public, but the rest is easily explored on foot and is particularly attractive around the Montagne de Vautubière, a ridge to the northwest of Rians which rises to well over 600 metres. But this tiny enclave is merely a prelude to the wild magnificence of the area immediately to the east, with the Gorges du Verdon and the Plateau de Valensole on its northern edge.

The best approach is by the northern branch of the road from Pertuis. Less than 10 kilometres from Vinon is the affluent town of Gréoux-les-Bains, whose population has multiplied nearly tenfold since the turn of the century, an increase due almost entirely to the exploitation of the town's thermal springs. Gréoux is said to derive its name from Gresilium, the water of pain, and there is evidence that the springs were used for their curative properties even in pre-Roman times. Evidence also suggests that these early settlers believed that the springs encouraged fertility, like the powers attributed to those around Aix-en-Provence. And there may be a connection with the curiously named chapel of Notre-Dame-des-Oeufs (Our Lady of the Eggs), just to the southeast of Gréoux, to which the infertile went in pilgrimage, a tradition now repeated on Easter Monday.

Whether either of these remedies was successful is not apparent. The modern population of Gréoux is predominantly elderly and well off, luxuriating in the white marble baths in the spa into which four million litres of bubbling sulphurous water gush daily. Jean Giono, who brought his own rheumatism here, once remarked – though this was before the town had taken on its present-day air of prosperity – that Gréoux was the best place he knew to cure boredom. Perhaps he was a connoisseur of tchatao, a kind of stew made primarily from aubergines and tomatoes and a very special permutation on the ubiquitous and very variable ratatouille.

From the centre of Gréoux, with its park and large sixteenth- and seventeenth-century houses (many of them designated as châteaux), a few hours' walk to the southeast, across the river, will bring you to wooded hills overlooking the reservoir behind the Barrage de Gréoux. The view from the point of land directly opposite the tiny lakeside resort of Esparron is particularly attractive. And it is relatively easy to reach any of the tiny hamlets on the lower slopes of the hills from this headland, or the attractive village of Saint-Julien. Here there is another subterranean curiosity – an interesting series of interconnecting cellars, many of them with two or three floors.

Between the southeastern end of the reservoir and Quinson just 6 kilometres further on, the Verdon cuts through a gorge which is over 500 metres deep in places. But this cleft pales in comparison with the Grand Canyon du Verdon some 25 kilometres to the northeast beyond the lake of Sainte Croix. This magnificent natural phenomenon can be easily reached by a quick road from Quinson to Riez and thence to Moustiers-Sainte-Marie. A more attractive way, however, is to follow the road from Gréoux along the valley of the Colostre. Just outside the village it runs through the Gorges du Colostre, with their distinctive red rock, and the villages of Saint-Martin-de-Brômes and the oddly named Allemagne-en-Provence.

Contrary to what some local people believe, the name Allemagne is not derived from the settlement of a Germanic tribe, nor from the residence of deserters from the German army during the Occupation. The most likely explanation is that Allemagne derives from *area magna* (from which Armagna), simply the designation of an open area on the southern edge of the Plateau de Valensole. An alternative theory is that it comes from Alemona, a fertility goddess. Although less likely, this derivation is both more attractive and nicely in keeping with traditions in Gréoux. Perhaps it

Above Tuiles romaines **in Gréoux.**

Right **All that remains of the first-century temple said to have been dedicated to Apollo at Riez.**

is also why the pretty château (begun in the late fourteenth century) and its grounds have been turned into a *colonie de vacances* for children.

Riez (pronounced Riess) lies only 10 kilometres further on along this narrow and intensively cultivated valley, a beautifully proportioned town sitting on a slight rise to the north of the river. Four granite columns in a field just to the south are said to have been part of a first-century temple to Apollo, and just opposite them is one of the oldest baptistries in France. Despite considerable restoration in the sixteenth century, the baptistry still retains its basic plan and features from 1200 years earlier. Square on the outside it is octagonal inside, with a cupola supported by eight elegant pillars in grey granite, topped by white capitals. In Riez itself large sections of the fourteenth-century town walls still stand, characterized by the large, smooth pebbles which were used in their construction. The town is typically Provençal, with vaulted passages and narrow streets and many fine buildings. One of the best is the Hôtel Mazan, a distinguished Renaissance house with an elegant staircase and some exquisite plaster-work. Not far away is the place Saint Antoine, worth visiting to see the inscription on its early nineteenth-century sundial, which has come directly from the heart of someone who must have worked long hours in the relentless heat of the Provençal summer: '*L'instant le plus serein est marqué par une ombre.*' ('The most peaceful moment is indicated by a shadow.')

Without the benefits brought by thermal springs, Riez has remained very unspoiled, twice as large as it was fifty years ago but with a relatively stable population of families who have been there for several generations. It is superbly placed, both in relation to the uplands of the plateau and for the amazing scenery of the Gorges du Verdon. The tiny village of Moustiers-Sainte-Marie, said by some to be the 'soul of Provence', should also be explored. Only a few kilometres away, it can be reached by one of two roads which climb up over a sharp little ridge of hills running north from the lake of Sainte Croix. (It is also possible to do the journey on foot by the *Grande Randonnée 4*, which takes a more southerly line.)

Although small, Moustiers has three claims to fame: its site, its *faïence*, and its traditions. Overlooking the valley of La Maire, the village is backed by a great wall of rock which appears to have been split open by a blow with a giant sword. Packed up against these mountains, Moustiers seems precarious and unstable, but its houses, arcades, tiny squares and arches make up one of the finest villages in Provence. And the twelfth-century church of Notre-Dame (expensively restored in 1928) has a magnificent square belfry on four floors. This is in what is known as the Lombardy style and is well worth comparing with the belfry at Saint-Trophime in Arles, or at the priory of Saint-Symphorien at Buoux in the Lubéron.

Moustiers has always been a peaceable village, probably largely because of its position. Its name is thought to derive from the Old French for a monastic community, *monastère*, of which there seem to have been several – hence the plural – from the fifth century. Evidence for medieval paper, cloth and pottery industries has been discovered here, but Moustiers' real fame dates from the seventeenth century and the development of *faïence*. This form of ceramics originated in Faenza in Italy, where it had been practised since the thirteenth century, and was introduced to Moustiers by Pierre Clérissy. The only colours used originally were blue and pale cream, but a wider range, coupled with more complex designs, was developed in the eighteenth century by Joseph Olérys, who learned the art in Spain. By the end of that century hundreds of thousands of pieces were being produced annually and distributed throughout Provence. The journey – by mule and then by boat on the then untamed and treacherous Durance – was not without considerable risk for such delicate ware.

During the nineteenth century the industry declined, but in the mid 1920s it was once more revived by the aptly named Marcel Provence and is

Moustiers-Sainte-Marie.

now thriving. This is partly because it has become something of a cult to collect pieces of *faïence de Moustiers*, especially anything antique. Much of the modern output is crafted with care, produced in delicate colours and with traditional pastoral scenes containing the occasional exotic bird or plant. But some of it is cheap and mass-produced. Imitations find their way into the stores of all the main cities at grossly inflated prices. Moustiers is full of invitations to visit *ateliers* and to buy direct, but care has to be taken to ensure you get the real thing and introductions from known and knowledgeable people are invaluable.

Of all the traditions and stories associated with Moustiers, probably the most intriguing is connected with the chapel of Notre-Dame-de-Beauvoir situated above the village, tucked in hard against the rocks and guarded by its twin cypress trees. In the fifth century the theologian Pierre Chrysologue had children brought to the chapel who had been still-born, or who had died before baptism, and whose spirits had therefore not gone to paradise. The children were momentarily brought back to life, baptised and thereby rescued from some kind of eternal limbo. This legend is commemorated by a pilgrimage and a mass (La Messe de l'Aurore) on 8 September, and is found as well at Notre-Dame-de-Nazareth in Carpentras and at Notre-Dame-de-Vie at Venasque.

From Moustiers the road winds down through the hamlet of Beauvoir with the face of the Plateau de Négaou to the east. Just after Beauvoir it forks. To the west lies the artificial lake of Sainte Croix, part of the massive hydro-electric scheme. This covers the village of Les Salles and is fed by the spring known as the Fontaine l'Evêque, which pumps out 5000 litres of water per second. After 10 kilometres the road forks again and the left-hand route winds up to Aiguines. This is generally noted only as the western access point to the Gorges du Verdon but it is worth visiting in its

Château de Saint-Clair to the south of Moustiers, overlooking the lake of Sainte Croix.

own right, especially in winter. The views south across the barren, windswept northwestern section of the Camp de Canjuers, white with snow, are distinctly eerie, and have justifiably been compared on a number of occasions with a lunar landscape. In the village itself notice the dumpy château with its round towers topped by multi-coloured tiles, or the Ferme de la Médecine, said to have sheltered the last recognized witch in Provence.

The main section of the gorge is just over 20 kilometres long. The whole area was first explored as recently as 1905 by Edouard Martel, but it was not exploited as a tourist attraction for another twenty-five years, and it was only with the construction of the Corniche Sublime in 1948 that the gorge could be easily reached by car. Since then many 'improvements' have been made, such as the addition of look-out points (*belvédères*) and picnic areas, but the road is frequently closed in winter by snow or black ice. The gorge marks a line of weakness along a massive geological fault which the river has gradually eroded away. The scenery is much wilder than anything found in the Ardèche or the Tarn and is arguably the finest in all Europe. The gorge is over 700 metres deep in places, its sides brilliant green with trees and bushes that thrive in the lush climate. This vegetation in turn supports an amazing insect life, and over sixty species of dragonflies have been recorded here. White and pale mauve rocks stand out against the vegetation and at the bottom is the river, a strip of dark jade green — apparently quiet but subject to violent floods, especially in the winter and spring.

Most modern visitors are content to follow the Corniche Sublime by car, weaving round safe but vertiginous bends of a kind they may never have experienced before. Beyond the Etroit des Cavaliers the road passes through the tunnel du Fayet, skirts the point of rock of the same name and reaches the point where the gorge is joined by the Canyon de l'Artuby. This deep cleft is crossed by a single-span bridge 110 metres long.

There is no access by road to the Canyon de l'Artuby and it gives a very good idea of what the whole area

Left Aiguines, with the lower Alps in the far distance.

Above The Gorges du Verdon, the most spectacular in Europe.

203

must have been like less than a century ago. Although on a smaller scale than the gorge, it is none the less hundreds of metres deep. In places it is only a metre or so wide at the bottom, it is scattered with huge blocks of rock throughout its length and is often quite dark. Exploration has to be done on foot and is not without danger. It is advisable to take a guide and this is true too of any expedition into the major Verdon gorge, even though it is possible to follow the *Grande Randonnée 4* from the Etroit des Cavaliers north to the Point Sublime along the *Sentier Martel*.

The landscape of this central point of Provence is moulded on such a vast scale that it defies description. Like the Mont Ventoux, its character changes abruptly with the weather; sublimely beautiful on a peaceful day in summer or autumn, it can be threatening and genuinely frightening during a storm or on a windy night. And it should never be forgotten that the gorges have been a great obstacle to economic and social development, separating two rural areas for centuries. Few people can have been tempted to make the dangerous descent of the gorge in order to cross one of the few bridges. And the only animals to have done so must have been the wild goats which still frequent the woods.

After the Pont de l'Artuby the road leaves the gorge, winding northeast to the tiny village of Trigance and then to the valley of the Jabron. The river is fringed by the magnificent trees of the Bois de Colle de Bries and the Bois de la Faye, through which the road runs to rejoin the northern route from Moustiers at the Pont de Soleils a few kilometres north. (There is a most attractive walk southwest from this point along clear tracks to the châteaux at Soleils and Valcros.) From here to Castellane the road follows the Verdon again as it sweeps round to the east in a narrow valley, the Porte de Saint Jean, overlooked by the chapels of Saint-Jean and Saint-Etienne.

Eight hundred metres above sea-level, Castellane gives the impression of being pinched between massive land formations. It is a perfect gap town and commands the Route Napoléon as it comes up from Grasse to the southeast. Here the climate and scenery are already much more alpine in quality. Immediately to the north the land rises steeply to around 1500 metres, there are signposts to ski-lifts and to small resorts, and snow poles at the sides of the road. Even at the height of summer the air is distinctly fresh and gullies may still have snow in them as late as April. But apart from the obvious strategic importance of its position, what characterizes Castellane is the extraordinary outcrop of rock 180 metres high just to the east of the village and topped by a seventeenth-century chapel. On several occasions in the past the local population retreated to this rock when under attack or as a refuge from floods. The Castellane family which originally occupied it gradually grew in importance and strength throughout the Middle Ages. In 1483 Louis XI, sensing a potential problem, ordered their castle to be destroyed, just as he had done at Les Baux. None the less, if not in any way a threat, Castellane continued to be the focus of many a political and religious dispute. For example, the noisy Fête des Pétardiers on 31 January commemorates Castellane's resistance to the Huguenots who laid siege to the village in 1586.

The road northwest from Castellane towards Digne follows the contours of steep, wooded hills until it joins the valley of the Asse. At this point there is a minor road leading southwest to Blieux, overlooked by the great mound of rock known as the Mourre de Chanier, which rises to nearly 2000 metres. Blieux is a curiosity. Only about fifty people live here (although there were a thousand in the eighteenth century) and, unless it is rescued by those in search of a really remote *résidence secondaire*, it may well be no more than ruins within twenty years or so. The same is true of Majastres just 4 kilometres to the northwest, but accessible from Blieux only on foot across a steep and difficult terrain which rises in places to over 1700 metres. Majastres' decline has been even more dramatic; there are only a dozen or so people living there today, eking out a barely basic existence from the

Castellane lies close to this great rock outcrop.

Blieux: remote but beautiful.

land. Appropriately enough, the name Majastres comes from the Latin *male jactus*, or badly situated. These two communities and a handful of others, often in ruins and once picturesquely described by Giono as looking like 'old wasps' nests', are the only settlements in this remote area – one of the most deserted parts of Provence, which most visitors never penetrate.

Those who come into Castellane by the southern route can complete a circular trip back to Moustiers by following the road which leads west from the Pont de Soleils. This passes through a tunnel in the very face of the cliff at the Clue de Carejuan and follows the line of the mountain round beneath the *village perché* of Rougon. At the Point Sublime the road crosses the *Grande Randonnée 4*; thereafter it leaves the gorge for the gentler countryside around La Palud-sur-Verdon, partly tree-covered (forests of Barbin and d'Aire), partly cultivated with lavender fields. A rewarding detour from this route is to take the minor road (D23)

that leads from the centre of Palud southwest along the Ravin de Mainmorte. It winds spectacularly through the mountains on the north side of the gorge, through the Belvédères de la Maline and then north along the Barre de l'Escalès to the wild and aptly named Chaos de Trescaire. At this point it turns sharply west back to La Palud, thus completing a small but worthwhile excursion.

The Ravin de Mainmorte and the whole area around La Palud is littered with the remains and memories of the civilizations and communities which have lived here since prehistoric times. Protected from the south and east by the gorge and with clear views to the north, the site of the village must have been virtually impregnable. In fact La Palud was originally built on the Montagne des Barris, where the site of the ruined village can still be seen. And north of the modern (fifteenth-century) site is Châteauneuf-lès-Moustiers on the crest of the Montdenier ridge, abandoned since the 1930s and now much vandalized, but still worth a visit for its atmospheric qualities.

Those who want to appreciate in full just how desolate and wild this area of upper Provence is should follow the path (the *sentier départemental 2*) from La Palud directly north through Châteauneuf, over the Montdenier hills to Majastres and on to the valley of the Asse and the Route Napoléon. This is a walk of about 30 kilometres, and though well marked it is physically quite a challenge. There can also be a strong feeling that you are intruding and it is possible to walk for hours without meeting anyone, or at best only the occasional shepherd and his dog. Above all this is sheep country. Although in many places sheep are now moved from one place to another by convoys of lorries, in May huge flocks come up into these hills from the lowlands to a fresher climate. Century-old trails (*drailles*), often no more than 10 or 20 metres wide, are followed instinctively by the animals and the whole complex operation seems both ritualistic and mysterious. The size of the flock is indicated by a special name: more than a thousand sheep is an *escabot*, a hundred or so a *bastoun d'avé* and a handful a *trentenier*. Not infrequently the sheep are led by goats.

The shepherd is a silent man. Isolation is what he is used to and he may spend hours merely gazing into the distance, whittling a stick. He will not make conversation unless pressed and yet he will be friendly and hospitable, sharing his bread and cheese (often made from goat's milk and over a year old, this is likely to be rock-hard, but it is deliciously creamy to taste).

In marked contrast to this spectacular and dramatic landscape beyond Moustiers and the Gorges du Verdon is the Plateau de Valensole, stretching away north to the valley of the Bléone and cut almost exactly in half by the Asse. From the valley of the Durance to the west the land rises gently to between 600 and 1000 metres. In geological terms the whole plateau – one of the biggest in France – is a crust of pudding-stone several hundred metres thick. Partly wooded, it is mostly divided into massive holdings of land, which are sometimes as large as 3000 hectares. There is a little fruit farming on the western edge, but the bulk of the plateau is given over to the cultivation of grain, olives, almonds and, above all, lavender. In winter row upon endless row of lavender bushes line the slopes like huge armies of dormant hedgehogs. In March the almond trees are speckled with white and pink blossom, and in July and August they form splashes of dark green against a sea of glorious mauve.

At harvest time at the height of summer the air is often heavy with the scent from lavender distilleries, whose coils of black smoke can be seen in all directions. The growing and initial distillation of lavender essence is, like the making of olive oil, more complicated than it might appear. The quality of plants varies. True lavender (*la lavande*) which grows on the high ground is best; *aspic* and *le lavandin* (a hybrid of *lavande* and *aspic*) are the most common and productive species, while there is also a common variety, no better than a weed despite its attractive deep purple flowers. Plants take three to four years to mature, though *le lavandin* has the commercial advantage of doing so more quickly. The right conditions of climate and soil are essential, and even then the effort seems disproportionate to the result. Tradition holds that the flowers are best picked under the rising sun, but such is the scale of operation that the precious stalks will be gathered all day and every day for three weeks.

Freak storms can be disastrous. In some places harvesting is still occasionally done by hand with a sickle and the stalks are left to dry at the edge of the fields in piles a metre deep. Once at the distillery, up to 300 kilos of lavender are then needed in order to produce a single kilo of essence! The whole process is hot, sticky and unpleasant, and the distilleries themselves, usually primitive constructions, are vastly different from the shining tubes and containers to be seen in the perfume factories at Grasse, where much of the essence finally goes. Competition from abroad and the use of synthetic materials for the manufacture of cheaper perfume increasingly pose a serious threat to the lavender growers. Any conversation in one of the cafés on the edge of Valensole will, after a hard day's harvesting, quickly turn to discontent.

South of the Asse valley, in places a kilometre wide with banks of sand and pebbles, the principal roads across the plateau run west-east following rivers such as the Vallongue or the Laval. Paths in this country are plentiful, hugging the contours of gently undulating hills. The two places of any size are Puimoisson, 11 kilometres north of Riez, and Valensole. Puimoisson's only claim to fame is a huge square shaded by lotus trees, but Valensole is much more rewarding.

In this 'land of the cold sun', as Alexandre Arnoux once called the plateau, Valensole is a delightful town. Paradoxically, while many smaller villages are suffering from depopulation, it is enjoying considerable expansion, with its native population swelled by commuters to the Manosque area, retired people and a number of *résidences secondaires*. Built on a site that was occupied by the Romans, there is also evidence for earlier settlement by a tribe known as the Variacens. Important administratively from the tenth century, Valensole belonged in part to the counts of Provence and in part to the abbey at Cluny in Burgundy. During the second half of the sixteenth century it suffered from religious disputes, but grew in the more peaceable climate of the next two hundred years.

Many attractive streets and houses remain from this period, part of the medieval *quartier* around the church of Saint-Blaise, and are now protected. And this is how Valensole will probably remain. Unlike Gréoux, or Digne further north, the town has no natural advantage to exploit other than its essential simplicity. Probably the village's last real claim to international fame was as the birthplace of Admiral Pierre de Villeneuve, who, defeated by Nelson at Trafalgar, promptly killed himself.

The northern half of the plateau is very similar to that around Valensole except that a larger area of it is

Above **Outside Puimoisson on the Plateau de Valensole.**

Right **The stony bed of the Bléone west of Digne.**

less accessible. (The Asse itself is only bridged at four places.) In the southwest corner, just above the confluence of the Asse and the Durance, lies the thriving village of Oraison. Like Valensole, it continues to grow in size, largely due to its involvement with the hydro-electric scheme and a thriving agricultural community. (The incongruity of its medieval château flanked by a modern swimming pool is a neat indication of contrasting values.) From Oraison a range of wooded hills about 3 kilometres wide, La Basse Montagne, runs up the west side of the plateau to Les Mées and can be crossed at various points by well-tended forest tracks. Some of the villages in the interior are slowly falling into ruins, but others still survive. Places of note include Puimichel with its tiled sepulchres and a fine eighteenth-century town house; Entrevennes overlooking the valley of the Rancure with its seventeenth-century rectangular château and two round towers; Bras-d'Asse which dates from the eighth century and is now being vigorously and tastefully restored; and the tiny hamlets of Saint-Jeannet, Ajonc or Espinouse. There are not so many roads here as south of the Asse, but paths are plentiful and, except in severe weather, provide pleasant walking.

Towards the northeast corner of the northern half of the plateau, the hills crowd in around the valley of the Bléone and Digne rather as they do around Castellane. Digne – or Digne-les-Bains as it used to be known – is a lively and attractive town owing much of its prosperity, like Gréoux, to thermal springs. These were certainly extensively used by the Romans and now attract thousands of visitors each year. (The baths were completely modernized in 1983.) But Digne also owes its importance to its position. Surrounded by forested hills and on the confluence of the Bléone, the Eaux-Chaudes and the Madaric, it is, like Sisteron, a natural gap town and a genuine transition point between Provence and the Alps. It appears to have been a capital in its own region long before the Romans arrived in 14 BC and conquered the local tribe, the Brodiontii. Like Castellane, Digne suffered a great deal from attacks and violence, especially during the late sixteenth century. Shortly after, in 1629, 85 per cent of the population died from the plague. Yet Digne managed to recover and is today one of the biggest and busiest of the inland towns of Provence.

In 1955, Eric Whelpton described Digne in the following terms in his book *The Road to Nice*: 'Apart from a tree-shaded walk near the river, Digne is not an attractive place, and its inhabitants do not appear to have a distinctive character. In the seventeenth and eighteenth centuries this place was a popular spa to which people came from afar to cure their gout or rheumatism. Doubtless they were encouraged to do so because of the incredible boredom of life in the country, and also because the climate here is mild in the autumn.' It is difficult to imagine how anyone could have held such a jaundiced view, but if what Whelpton says was true in the 1950s, it certainly is not so now. Quite apart from the activity generated by the *établissement thermal*, Digne has long been recognized as the lavender capital of Provence. A massive fair is held at the end of August, while earlier, on the first Sunday of the same month, the *fête de la lavande* is celebrated with a magnificent floral procession. The town is also very active culturally, rivalling both Aix and Avignon with its regular concerts, poetry readings and exhibitions. A symposium on sculpture is held in odd years, alternating with one on engraving. And there is a permanent exhibition relating to the geology of the region, including books from one of the best collections on the subject in France.

Nor is Digne without places of historical interest. It is still worth visiting the quartier du Rochas with its narrow, twisting streets and seeing the exquisite plaster-work in the seventeenth-century Hôtel Thoron de la Robine. Another building of note is the former cathedral of Notre-Dame-du-Bourg, whose one-time bishop Bienvenu Myriel was immortalized by Victor Hugo in his novel *Les Misérables*. This slate-blue

---

Lavender plants near Digne, like thousands of sleeping hedgehogs.

211

building originated in the eleventh century, though it is claimed to be on the site of an earlier church. (The white marble altar has been dated to the fifth century, but it may have been brought to Digne from elsewhere.) The cathedral has three particularly exceptional features: a fine and complex wrought-iron belfry; a fourteenth-century rose window; and a large number of wall paintings, a whole series of which deals dramatically with the themes of vice and virtue. An added attraction is that Digne is at the end of one of the most attractive and popular railway journeys in Provence. For the less energetic the Digne-Nice line (150 kilometres in just over three hours) provides a very good introduction to villages such as Entrevaux or Saint-André-les-Alpes and to the valleys of the Asse, Verdon and Var.

From Digne the fastest route back to Sisteron follows the Bléone west to Malijai and then turns north to cross the Durance at Château-Arnoux. But Digne itself is a good centre for a variety of excursions into the immediate area round about. To the southeast above the valley of the Eaux-Chaudes is Entrages, from which a difficult path leads up to the Sommet de Causson and thereafter to the chapel of Saint-Michel at well over 1500 metres. From here the views across Digne and the Bléone northwest towards Sisteron are superb. So too are those from Les Dourbes, just 6 kilometres northeast under the edge of the Montagne de Coupe, or from Les Hautes-Sieyes across the Bléone. This is magnificent walking country, particularly in the spring, but for those who prefer to travel by car the mountains to the north can be reached along the valley of Le Bès from Digne, or by way of that of Les Duyes, half-way between Digne and Malijai.

A slower but more interesting way to return to Sisteron is by way of the road to the south of the Bléone. After some unattractive suburbs outside Digne, this runs under the escarpment of forested hills which eventually meet La Basse Montagne on the western edge of the plateau. There is quite easy access to this country, especially on foot, with ruined dwellings from time to time recalling lost communities, as at La Signorette, Lagremuse and Chénerilles. Those who take this route should find the time to visit Gaubert, just 5 kilometres from Digne, where tombs around the ruined church have been carved directly out of the rocks. Eventually the minor road rejoins the Route Napoléon at Malijai, on the edge of a large area dominated by hydro-electric stations and an aerodrome. Already busy, it will presumably become even more so once the projected motorway has been completed. Fortunately it is possible to cover the last 15 kilometres to Sisteron on the east side of the Durance through Volonne and Salignac along a strip of intensively farmed land – a final reminder of how agriculture remains essential to the economy, even in an area of advanced technological development.

No-one should leave Provence without seeing a massive reminder of another departure, centuries ago. Between Malijai and Les Mées to the southwest is a line of pointed rocks, some over 100 metres high, known as Les Pénitents des Mées. They are most striking either in the early spring, when the white stone stands out against a background of pines browned by frost, or when bathed in moonlight. Geologically they are somewhat unromantically described in French as *gigantesques poudingues*! Legend, however, is more colourful. During the wars against the Saracens the monks of Saint-Donat took shelter in the Lure mountains. They prayed that the local lord, Sire de Bevon, would defeat the invaders, which he did, but he also captured the Saracens' harem. Donat begged him to send such temptresses away and de Bevon duly arranged to despatch them to Arles by boat. The monks came down from the hills to oversee the operation but were so disturbed at the mere sight of the beautiful Arab women that all modesty was forgotten. Donat was horrified by their behaviour and instantly turned his fellow monks into stone.

And there they still stand, their cowls lowered in shame.

Above Volonne, where the rocks appear almost liquid in some lights.

Index

215